Robert Lowry

Gospel Music

A choice collection of hymns and melodies new and old for gospel, revival, prayer and social meetings, family worship

Robert Lowry

Gospel Music

A choice collection of hymns and melodies new and old for gospel, revival, prayer and social meetings, family worship

ISBN/EAN: 9783337083700

Printed in Europe, USA, Canada, Australia, Japan

Cover: Foto ©Lupo / pixelio.de

More available books at **www.hansebooks.com**

GOSPEL MUSIC.

A CHOICE COLLECTION OF

HYMNS AND MELODIES

NEW AND OLD

FOR

GOSPEL, REVIVAL, PRAYER AND SOCIAL MEET-
INGS, FAMILY WORSHIP, Etc.

"*Speaking to yourselves in psalms and hymns and spiritual songs, sing-
ing and making melody in your hearts to the Lord.*"—*Eph. v: 19:*
"*Joy and gladness shall be found therein, thanksgiving, and the
voice of melody.*"—*Is. li: 3.*

BY

Rev. ROBERT LOWRY AND W. HOWARD DOANE.

NEW YORK AND CHICAGO:
Published by BIGLOW & MAIN,
Successors to WM. B. BRADBURY,
76 EAST NINTH ST., N. Y., 91 WASHINGTON ST., CHICAGO.
FOR SALE BY BOOKSELLERS GENERALLY.

Dedication.

THIS VOLUME IS AFFECTIONATELY INSCRIBED TO OUR CO-WORKER,
MR. H. THANE MILLER,
BY THE AUTHORS.

PREFACE.

The Ministerial Association of Cincinnati, early in January of this year, inaugurated a series of Union Evangelistic Meetings, and the author of SONGS OF DEVOTION was invited to *conduct* the music. The necessity was at once felt of having a collection of *Gospel music* that could be placed in the hands of every attendant at these services, and be of such a varied character, both as to words and music, as would draw the hearts of Christians "Nearer to God," and at the same time awaken the impenitent—songs that would tell "The Old, Old Story"—songs that would quicken the earnest Christian to "Come and Work for Jesus," and "Rescue the Perishing." This collection is now sent forth with the sincere hope and prayer that multitudes, by the blessing of God, through this instrumentality, may be led to pray to be "More Like Jesus," and each one in the heart to feel "I need Thee every Hour," and to exercise saving faith in Christ as their Redeemer, seek comfort and guidance of the *Holy Spirit*, and be brought to know of the great love of God to all mankind.

THE AUTHORS.

CINCINNATI, *February 5th*, 1877.

ELECTROTYPED AT
FRANKLIN TYPE FOUNDRY,
CINCINNATI.

☞ No one will be allowed to print or publish any of the Copyrighted Hymns or Tunes contained in this book, without the written permission of the publishers.

BIGLOW & MAIN.

GOSPEL MUSIC.

Praise ye the Lord. Sing unto the Lord a new song, and praise him in the congregation of saints.—Ps. cxlix : 1.

No. 1.   SWEET MOMENTS OF PRAYER.

"There I will meet with Thee and commune."—Exod. xxv : 22.

W. H. DOANE, by per.

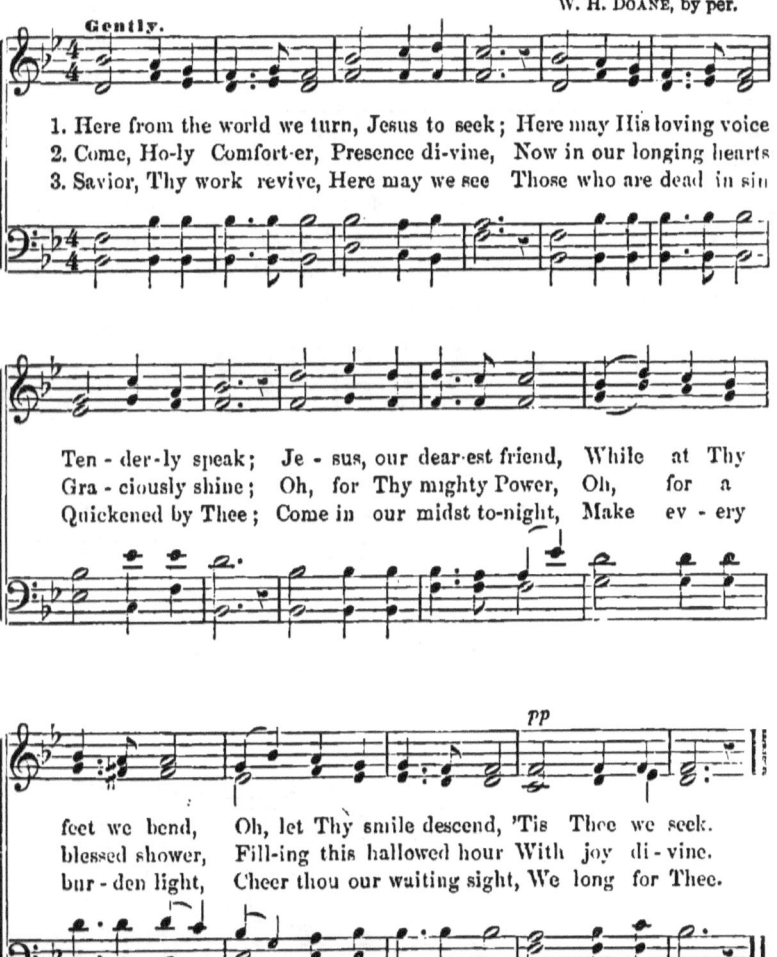

1. Here from the world we turn, Jesus to seek; Here may His loving voice Ten-der-ly speak; Je - sus, our dear-est friend, While at Thy feet we bend, Oh, let Thy smile descend, 'Tis Thee we seek.
2. Come, Ho-ly Comfort-er, Presence di-vine, Now in our longing hearts Gra - ciously shine; Oh, for Thy mighty Power, Oh, for a blessed shower, Fill-ing this hallowed hour With joy di - vine.
3. Savior, Thy work revive, Here may we see Those who are dead in sin Quickened by Thee; Come in our midst to-night, Make ev - ery bur - den light, Cheer thou our waiting sight, We long for Thee.

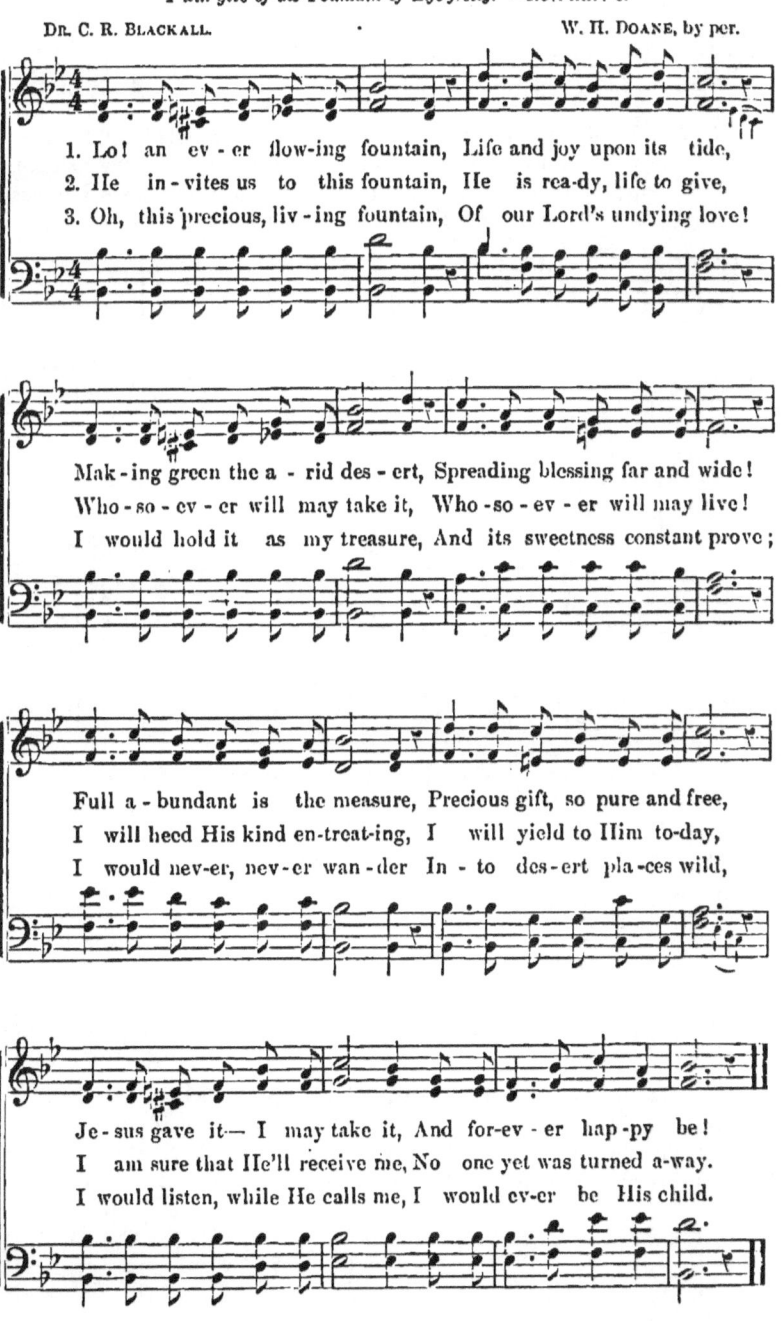

No. 4. ONLY JESUS.

"Besides me there is no Savior."—Isa. xliii: 11.

W. H. DOANE, by per.

1. On-ly Je-sus for my Sav-ior, He has shed His blood for me;
2. Ladened with my grief and sad-ness, Fearing, doubting, long I sighed,
3. Building on that Rock of A-ges, Soon were hushed my sad alarms;
4. En-ter in, thou might-y Lead-er; Ev-er-more my Captain be;

Long by sin a captive ta-ken, Jesus' love has set me free;
Till I found a ray of glad-ness—I had sinned, but Christ had died.
Tho' the storm a-round me rag-es, He a-lone my spir-it calms.
My Di-rect-or, Guid-er, Feed-er, Let me feel my strength in Thee.

On-ly Je-sus, On-ly Je-sus Can my great Redeem-er be;
"On-ly Je-sus, On-ly Je-sus," Then my broken spir-it cried;
On-ly Je-sus, On-ly Je-sus—I am safe within His arms;
On-ly Je-sus, On-ly Je-sus Can be all in all to me;

On-ly Je-sus, On-ly Je-sus Can my great Redeem-er be.
"On-ly Je-sus, On-ly Je-sus," Then my broken spir-it cried.
On-ly Je-sus, On-ly Je-sus—I am safe with-in His arms.
On-ly Je-sus, On-ly Je-sus Can be all in all to me.

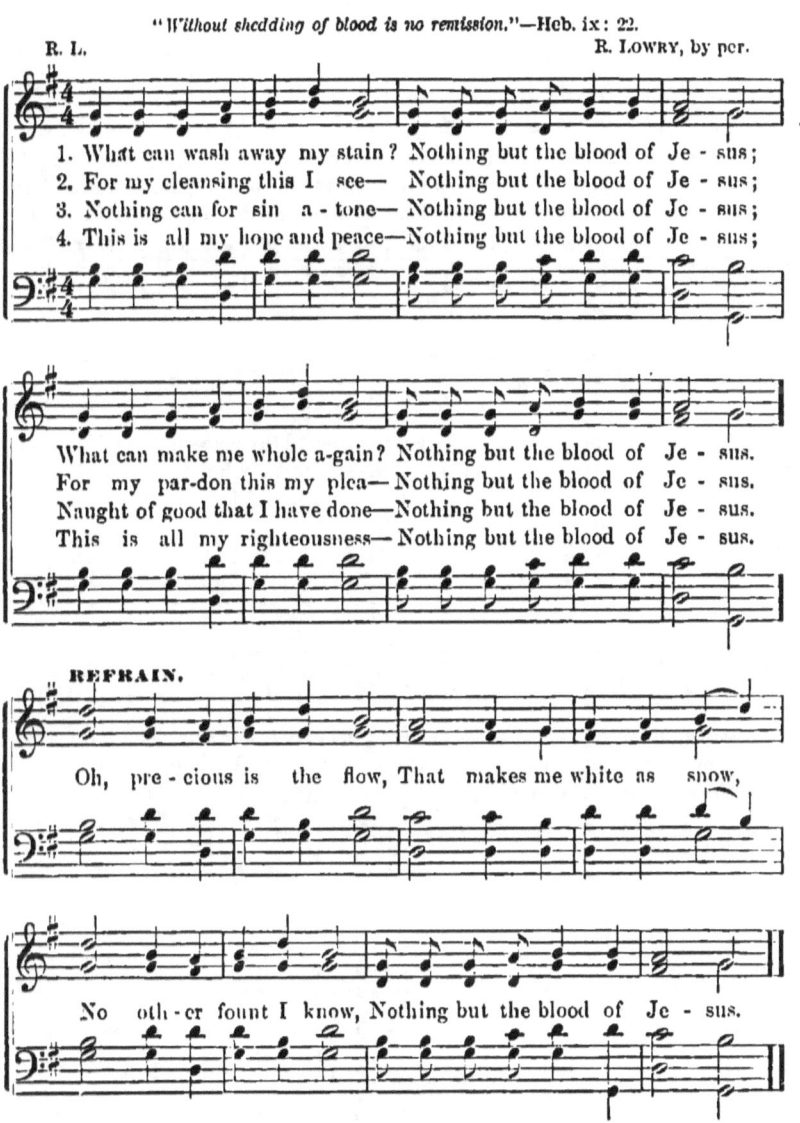

No. 7. NOTHING BUT THE BLOOD OF JESUS.

"Without shedding of blood is no remission."—Heb. ix: 22.

R. L. R. LOWRY, by per.

1. What can wash away my stain? Nothing but the blood of Je-sus;
   What can make me whole a-gain? Nothing but the blood of Je-sus.
2. For my cleansing this I see— Nothing but the blood of Je-sus;
   For my par-don this my plea— Nothing but the blood of Je-sus.
3. Nothing can for sin a-tone— Nothing but the blood of Je-sus;
   Naught of good that I have done—Nothing but the blood of Je-sus.
4. This is all my hope and peace—Nothing but the blood of Je-sus;
   This is all my righteousness— Nothing but the blood of Je-sus.

REFRAIN.

Oh, pre-cious is the flow, That makes me white as snow,
No oth-er fount I know, Nothing but the blood of Je-sus.

5 Now by this I'll overcome—
Nothing but the blood of Jesus;
Now by this I'll reach my home—
Nothing but the blood of Jesus.

6 Glory! glory! thus I sing—
Nothing but the blood of Jesus;
All my praise for this I bring—
Nothing but the blood of Jesus.

No. 9.   THERE'S A GENTLE VOICE.

"*Hearken to my voice.*"—Exod. xviii: 19.

W. H. Doane, by per.

1. There's a gen-tle voice with-in calls a-way, (calls a-way,) 'Tis a
   warning I have heard o'er and o'er, (o'er and o'er;)
   But my heart is melt-ed now, I o-bey, (I o-bey,) From my
   Sav-ior I will wander no . . . . more. } Yes, I will go,

2. He has promised all my sins to for-give, (to for-give,) If I
   ask in simple faith for His love, (for His love;)
   In His ho-ly word I learn how to live, (how to live,) And to
   la-bor for His kingdom a - - - - - - - bove. } Yes, I will go,

CHORUS.

yes, I will go; To Je-sus I will go and be saved;
Yes, I will go, yes, I will go; To Je-sus I will go and be saved.

3 I will try to bear the cross in my youth,
   And be faithful to its cause till I die;
  If with cheerful step I walk in the truth,
   I shall wear a starry crown by and by.

4 Still the gentle voice within calls away,
   And its warning I have heard o'er and o'er;
  But my heart is melted now, I obey;
   From my Savior I will wander no more.

No. 10. SAVE, OR I PERISH.

"And they came unto Him, and awoke Him, saying, Master, Master, we perish."—Luke viii: 24.

FANNY CROSBY.   W. H. DOANE, by per.

1. Wrecked on the billow, Rent by the gale, Parted the anchor, Shattered the sail. Faint and despair-ing Thus was my cry, Mas-ter, I per-ish, Save, or I die. Friend of the friendless, Where shall I flee? I have no ref-uge, On-ly in Thee; Leave me not hope-less, Hear Thou my cry, Master, I per-ish, Save, or I die.

2. Why am I faithless? Je-sus is near, Stilling the tempest, Chiding my fear, Bid-ding the wa-ters, Tur-bid and wild, Sleep in their beau-ty Calm as a child. Why am I faithless? Let me be-lieve, All that is need-ful I shall re-ceive; Thou that hast led me Safe thro' the storm, All Thou hast promised Thou wilt perform.

3. Oh, that my spirit Ever might rest Under Thy shadow Tranquil and blest, Fold-ing its pin-ions Lov-ing-ly there, Praising Thy goodness, Trusting Thy care! Friend of the friendless, Where shall I flee? I have no ref-uge, On-ly in Thee. Leave me not hope-less, Hear Thou my cry, Master, I per-ish, Save, or I die.

No. 11. THE HALF CAN NEVER BE TOLD.

"The half was never told me."—1 Kings x: 7.

W. H. D., by per.

1. God's ten-der mer-cy far exceeds The utmost power of thought;
2. His good-ness still prolongs my life, And fol-lows all my way,
3. O wond'rous grace that saves me now, The gift of God to me,
4. A-maz-ing, con-descending love, That can-cels all my sin;
5. When safe at home with Christ, our Lord, Among the saints a-bove,

That mer-cy from the brink of woe My wand'ring soul hath brought.
And grants me blessings from a-bove More plenteous ev-ery day.
How shall I praise Him for a gift So boundless, full and free.
I would proclaim Thy matchless power, But where shall I be-gin?
The half can nev-er then be told, Of ev-er-last-ing love.

REFRAIN.

The half can never be told, The half can nev-er be told,
The half can nev-er, can nev-er be told, can told,
My soul with rapture cries aloud, The half can never be told.
never be told,

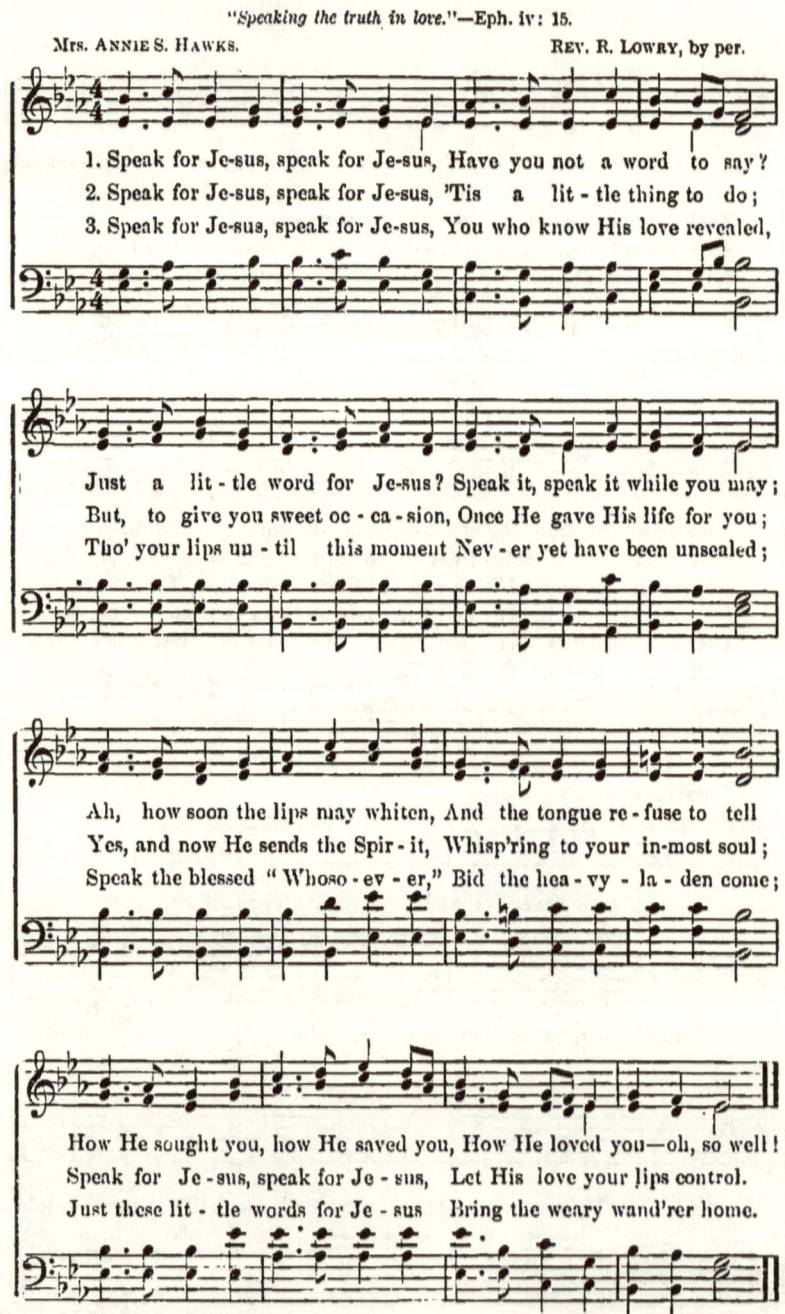

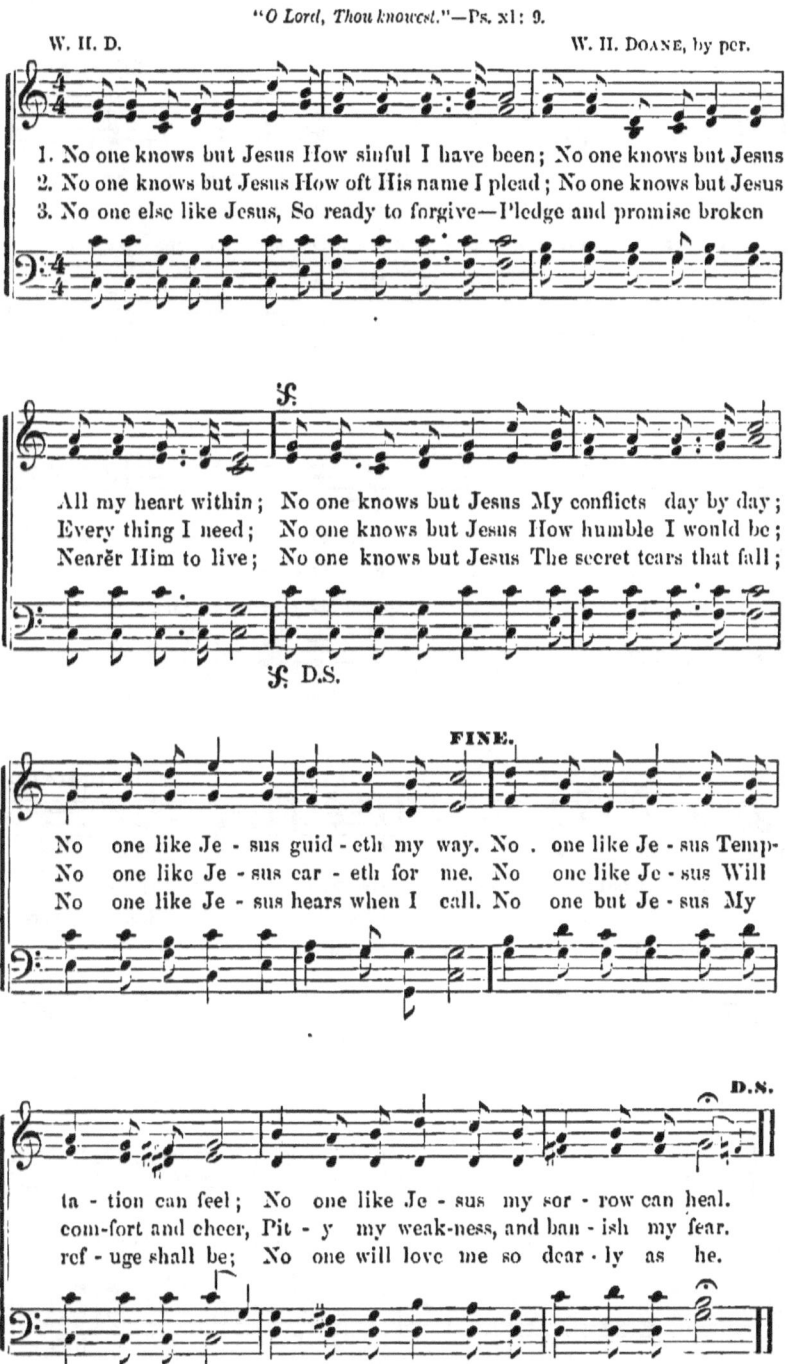

No. 14.   OVERFLOWING EVER.

"With thee is the fountain of life."—Psa. xxxvi: 9.

E. F. C. H.   R. Lowry, by per.

1. Lo! a fount-ain full and free, O-ver-flow-ing ev-er;
2. List the mur-mur that it speaks, O-ver-flow-ing ev-er;
3. Bless-ed fount! the pur-est known, O-ver-flow-ing ev-er;

Faint-ing heart, it is for thee, O-ver-flow-ing ev-er;
On the soul in song it breaks, O-ver-flow-ing ev-er;
Stream of life from out God's throne, O-ver-flow-ing ev-er;

REFRAIN.

Gushing, sparkling, nev-er still, Taste its sweetness, drink thy fill.
Sing-ing, soothing souls to ease, Mu-sic of all mel-o-dies.   O-ver-
Sa-cred blood for sinners spilt, This can cleanse away thy guilt.

flow-ing, o-verflow-ing ev-er, O-ver-flowing, Flowing now for thee.

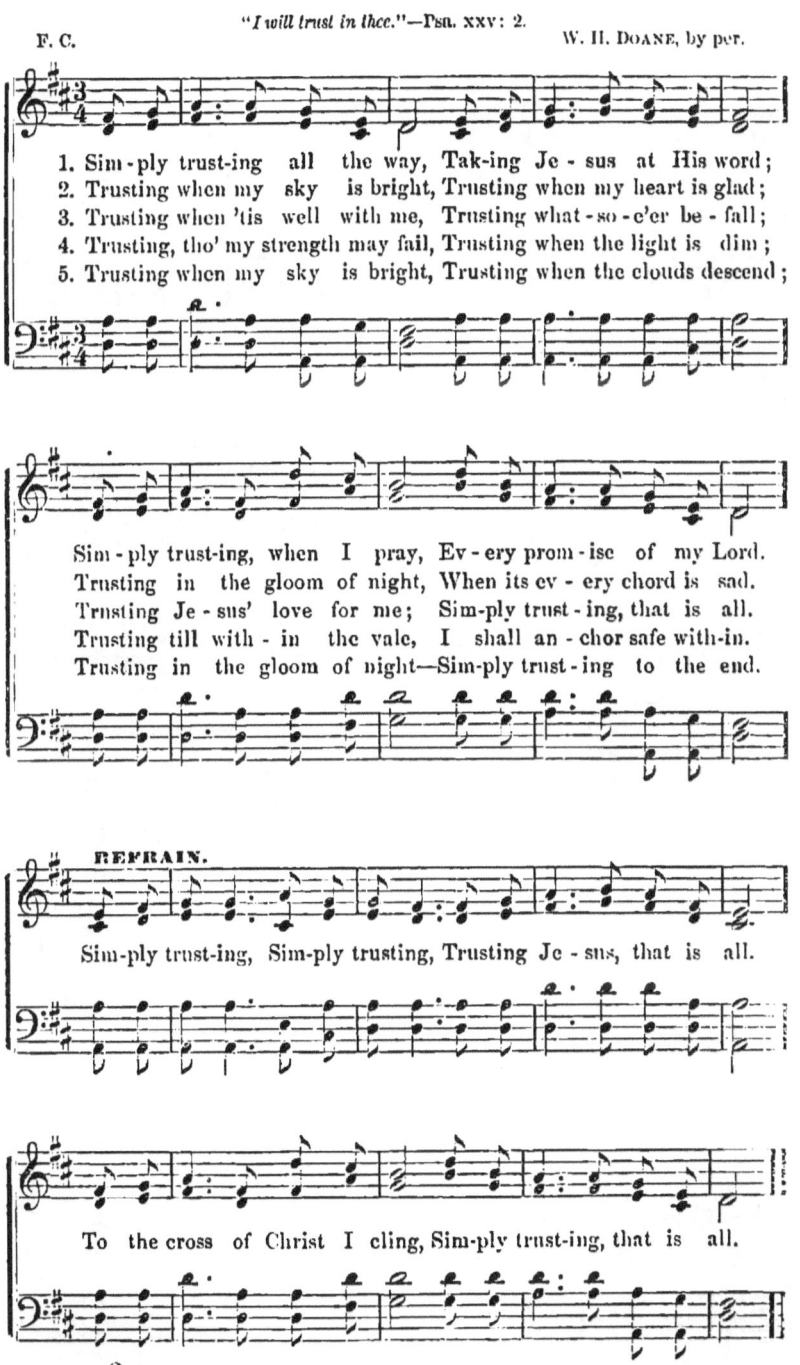

No. 17. TILL THE SAVIOR COMES.

Miss Kate Smiley.   *"I will come again."*—John xiv: 3.   W. H. Doane, by per.

DUET. Sop. and Tenor.   **CHORUS.**

1. Bright till our Lord's re-turn-ing, Till the Sav-ior comes;
2. Why should our hearts grow wea-ry Till the Sav-ior comes?
3. Watch, while our bur-den bear-ing, Till the Sav-ior comes;
4. Count ev-ery pain a pleas-ure, Till the Sav-ior comes;
5. Love be our joy-ful sto-ry, Till the Sav-ior comes,—

DUET.   **CHORUS.**

Oh, may our lamps be burn-ing, Till the Sav-ior comes.
Why should our way be drea-ry Till the Sav-ior comes?
Pray, while our la-bor shar-ing, Till the Sav-ior comes.
Trust for our heavenly treas-ure Till the Sav-ior comes.
Love and our home in glo-ry, Till the Sav-ior comes.

FULL CHORUS.

Here in sweet com-mun-ion, Watching, wait-ing ev-er,
Let us dwell in bonds of un-ion Till the Sav-ior comes.

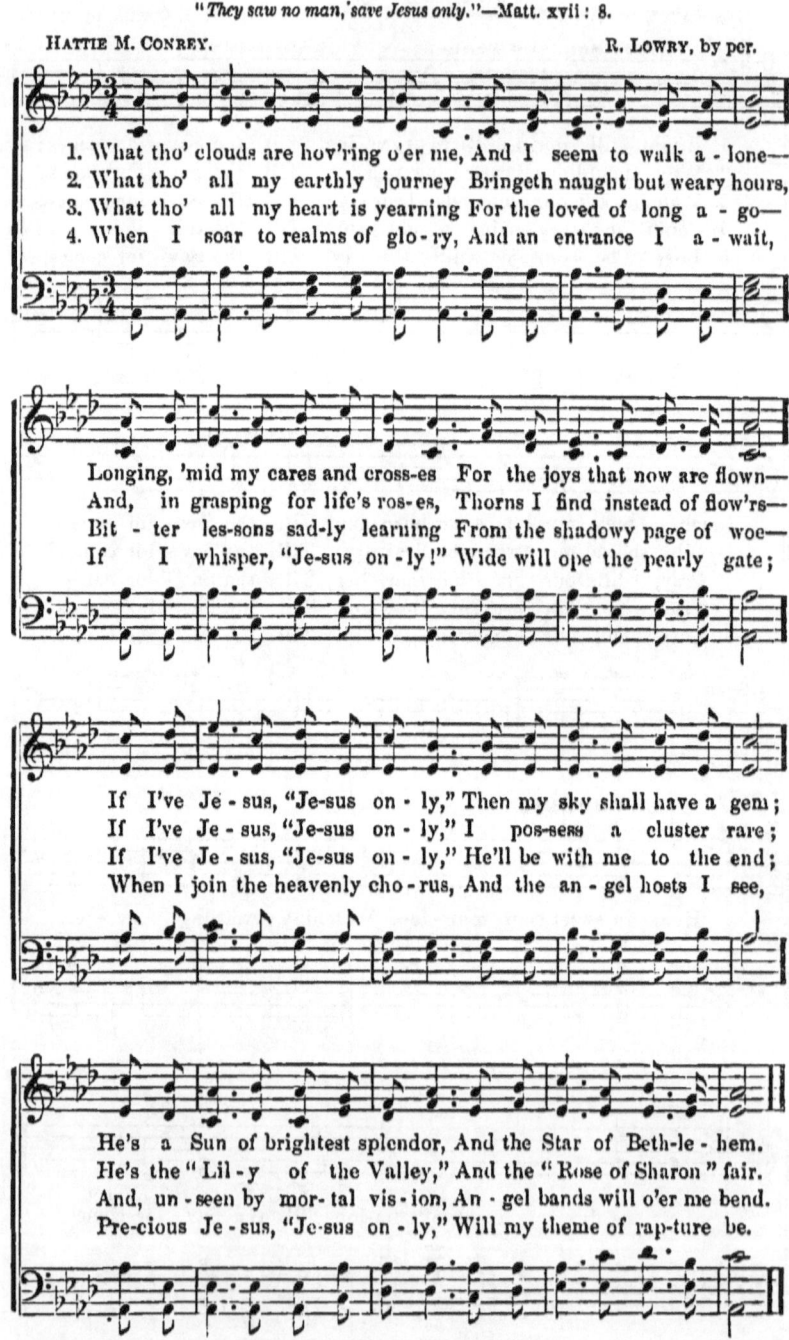

No. 19. JUST A WORD FOR JESUS.

"Will thou not tell."—Ezek. xxiv: 19.

FANNY J. CROSBY. W. H. DOANE, by per.

1. Now just a word for Je-sus; Your dearest friend so true;
2. Now just a word for Je-sus; You feel your sins forgiven,
3. Now just a word for Je-sus; A cross it can not be
4. Now just a word for Je-sus; Let not the time be lost;
5. Now just a word for Je-sus; And if your faith be dim,

Come, cheer our hearts and tell us What He has done for you.
And by His grace are striv-ing To reach a home in heaven
To say I love my Sa-vior Who gave His life for me.
The heart's neglect-ed du-ty Brings sor-row to its cost.
A-rise in all your weakness, And leave the rest to Him.

REFRAIN.

Now just a word for Je-sus, 'Twill help us on our way;

One lit-tle word for Je-sus, Oh, speak, or sing, or pray.

No. 20. ANYWHERE WITH THEE.

"Every man shall receive according to his labor."—1 Cor. iii: 8.

W. H. DOANE, by per.

1. Master, in the vineyard of Thy love, Hast Thou not a place for me?
2. I may tell a wear-y, fainting soul, Of the crimson fountain side,
3. Tho' among the thorns Thou bid'st me toil, If Thy hand direct me there,
4. Kindly words like precious seed doth fall, I may scatter as I go;

Wheresoe'er Thy guardian spirit leads, Gladly there I will fol-low Thee.
I may bring a wanderer to the cross, Precious cross, where the Savior died.
I shall know my work is not in vain, While the light of Thy love I see.
Cheered and strengthened by the dew of prayer, Golden fruit from the germ may grow.

REFRAIN.

A-ny-where to la-bor, Lord, for Thee, A-nywhere, a-nywhere, sweet 'twill be, Anywhere to labor, Lord, for Thee, Only comfort me.

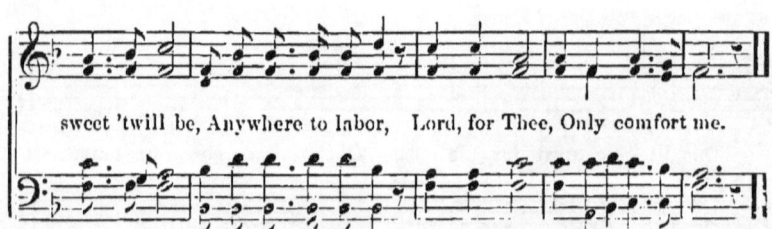

No. 21. LINGER NO LONGER.

"Therefore will the Lord wait, that he may be gracious unto you."—Isa. xxx: 18.

R. LOWRY, by per.

1. Ling-er no longer; Mercy is waiting for thee; Sin will grow stronger;
Now from its ty-ran-ny flee; The world that is smil-ing, so cheerful and gay, From Je-sus is lead-ing thee far-ther a-way.

2. Wealth without measure, Honor and fame thou may'st see; No earthly treasure
Ev-er can sat-is-fy thee; Thy rich-est pos-ses-sions de-lusive will prove, But wealth that en-dur-eth is laid up a-bove.

3. Tho' like a mountain, Sin on thy conscience should be, Come to the fountain
Opened at Cal-va-ry; Thou needest no lon-ger from hap-pi-ness roam, The Sav-ior is wait-ing to wel-come thee home.

REFRAIN.

Turn from thy straying, No longer delaying; Heaven opens for thee—
Turn from thy straying, No longer delaying; Heaven opens for thee.

No. 22. ONLY A STEP TO JESUS.

"Then come thou, for there is peace."—1 Sam. xx: 21.

FANNY J. CROSBY.   W. H. DOANE, by per.

1. On-ly a step to Jesus! Then why not take it now?
2. On-ly a step to Jesus! Be-lieve, and thou shalt live;
3. On-ly a step to Jesus! A step from sin to grace;
4. On-ly a step to Jesus! Oh, why not come and say,

Come, and, thy sin con-fess-ing, To Him, thy Sav-ior, bow.
Lov-ing-ly now He's wait-ing, And read-y to for-give.
What hast thy heart de-cid-ed? The moments fly a-pace.
Glad-ly to Thee, my Sav-ior, I give my-self a-way.

REFRAIN.

On-ly a step, On-ly a step, Come, He waits for Thee:
Come, and, thy sin con-fess-ing, Thou shalt receive a bless-ing,
Do not re-ject the mer-cy He free-ly of-fers thee.

No. 24.   GLAD TIDINGS.

"Shewing the glad tidings of the kingdom of God."—Luke viii: 1.

R. LOWRY, by per.

1. Glad tidings! glad tidings! Oh, wonder-ful love! A mes-sage has come from our Fa-ther a-bove; 'Tis Je-sus who brings it to young and to old, A message of mercy more precious than gold.

2. He saith to the wea-ry, Oh, come un-to me; The poor and the low-ly His glo-ry may see; He bless-eth the meek with His soul-cheering voice; He comforts the mourners and bids them re-joice.

3. How happy are they who be-lieve in the Lord, And love the sweet coun-sel they find in His word; Be read-y to hear and be swift to o-bey, And fol-low His track in the bright shining way.

REFRAIN.

Glad ti - - dings, glad ti - - dings! Oh, won-der-ful
glad tidings, glad ti-dings, glad ti-dings, glad ti-dings,

won-der-ful, won-der-ful love! Glad ti - - dings, glad
Glad ti-dings, glad ti-dings, glad

GLAD TIDINGS. Concluded.

ti - - dings! We hail the glad ti-dings of won-der-ful love.
tidings, glad tidings!

No. 25.   **IN TIME OF NEED.**

"Find grace to help in time of need."—Heb. iv: 16.

JOSEPHINE POLLARD.   R. LOWRY, by per.

1. Were it not for Thee, my Savior, Were it not for Thee, Advo-cate and
2. Were it not for that love and mercy With my Lord abide, When my conscience
3. Were it not that Thou hast promised Freely to forgive, In the face of
4. If there were no cross uplifted High on Cavalry, There would be no

CHORUS.

In - ter - ces - sor, Where would I be?
is o'er - tak - en, Where should I hide? How could I do without Thee,
my transgressions How could I live?
hope of par-don, No heaven for me.

Savior and friend? Thou art my on - ly ref - uge Safe to the end.

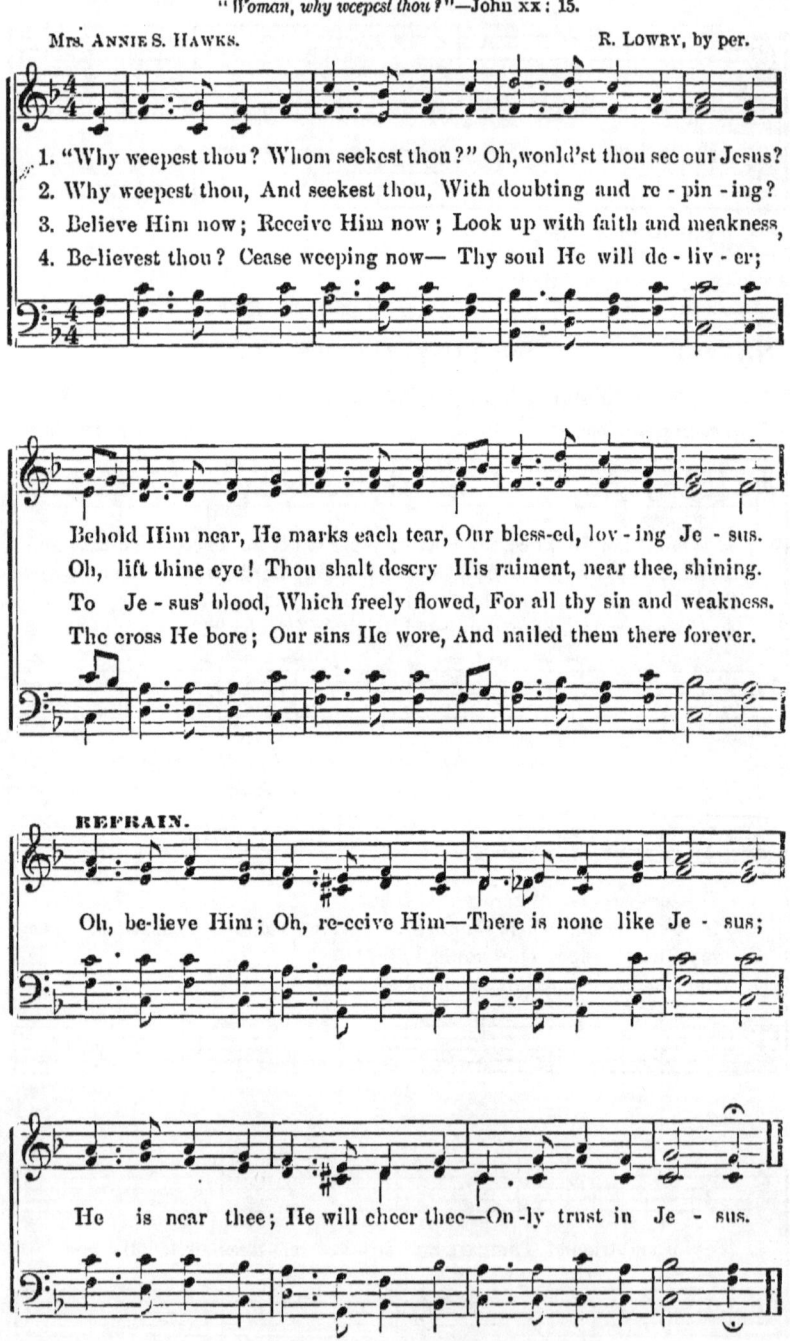

No. 27. I WILL GO AND TELL MY SAVIOR.

"And him that cometh to me I will in nowise cast out."—John vi: 57.

W. H. DOANE, by per.

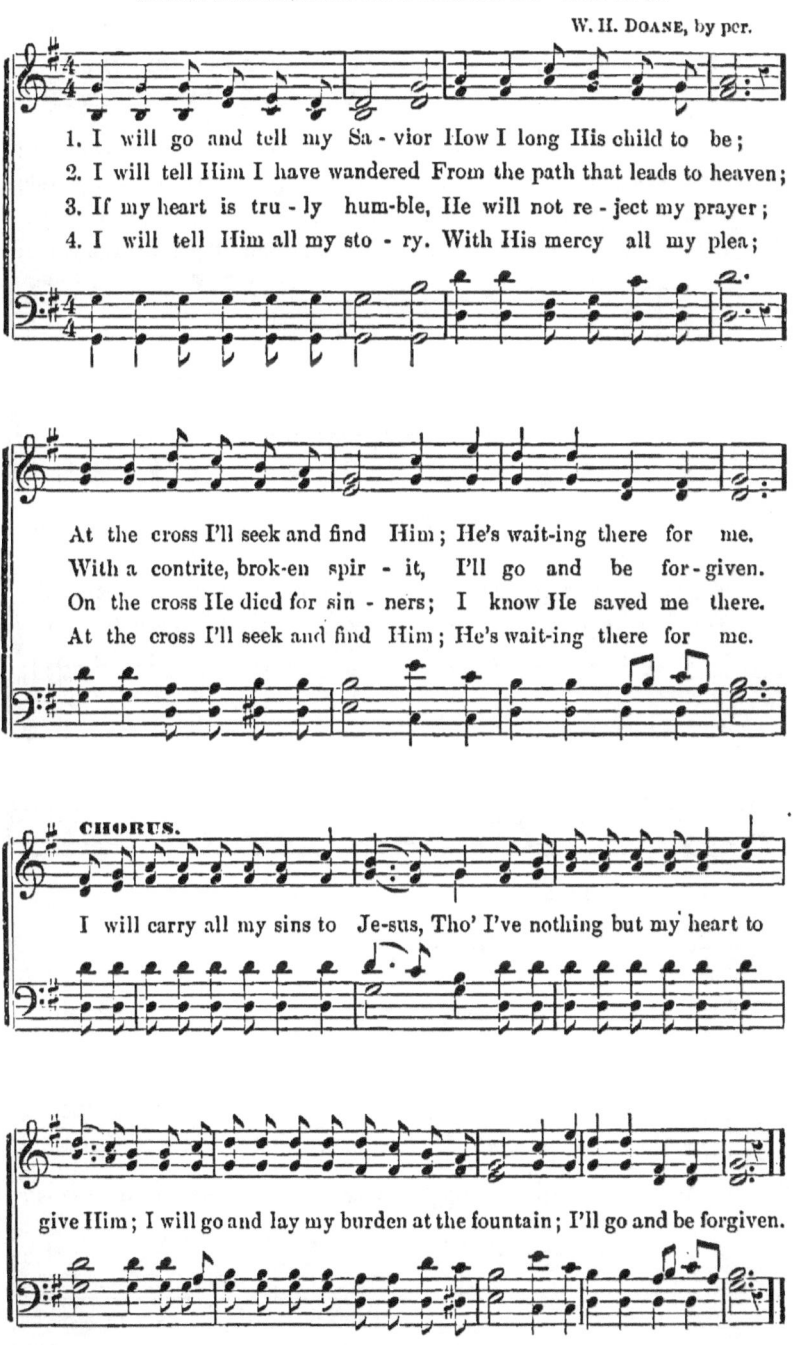

1. I will go and tell my Sa-vior How I long His child to be;
2. I will tell Him I have wandered From the path that leads to heaven;
3. If my heart is tru-ly hum-ble, He will not re-ject my prayer;
4. I will tell Him all my sto-ry, With His mercy all my plea;

At the cross I'll seek and find Him; He's wait-ing there for me.
With a contrite, brok-en spir-it, I'll go and be for-given.
On the cross He died for sin-ners; I know He saved me there.
At the cross I'll seek and find Him; He's wait-ing there for me.

CHORUS.

I will carry all my sins to Je-sus, Tho' I've nothing but my heart to give Him; I will go and lay my burden at the fountain; I'll go and be forgiven.

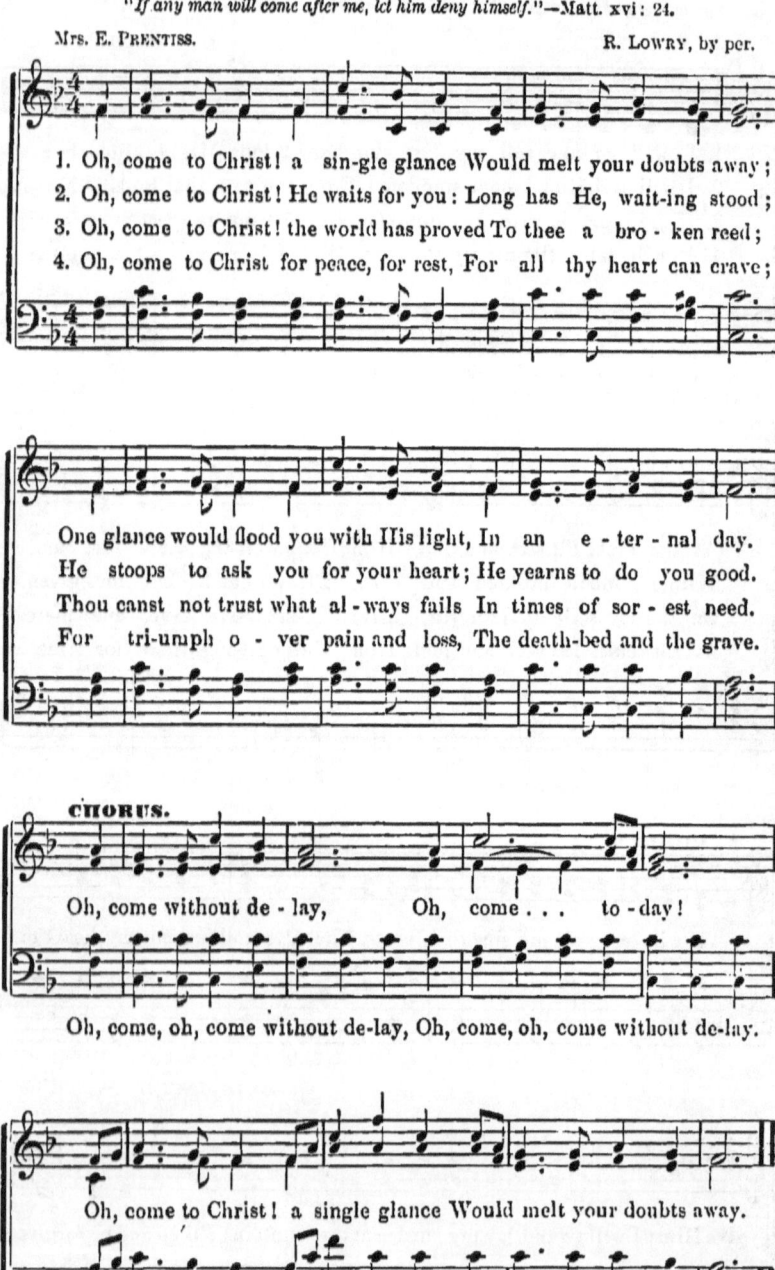

No. 30. DRAW ME NEARER.

"Let us draw near with a true heart."—Heb. x: 22.

FANNY J. CROSBY.   W. H. DOANE, by per.

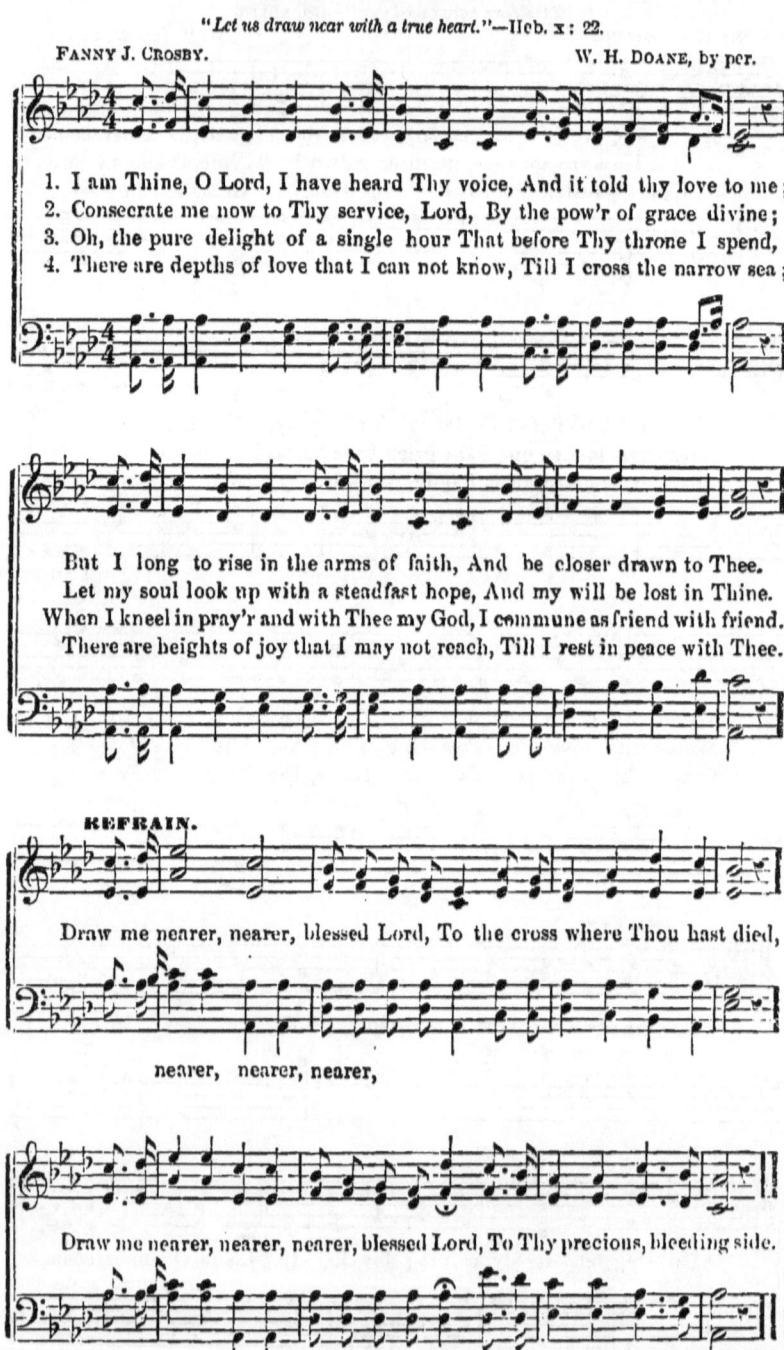

1. I am Thine, O Lord, I have heard Thy voice, And it told thy love to me;
2. Consecrate me now to Thy service, Lord, By the pow'r of grace divine;
3. Oh, the pure delight of a single hour That before Thy throne I spend,
4. There are depths of love that I can not know, Till I cross the narrow sea;

But I long to rise in the arms of faith, And be closer drawn to Thee.
Let my soul look up with a steadfast hope, And my will be lost in Thine.
When I kneel in pray'r and with Thee my God, I commune as friend with friend.
There are heights of joy that I may not reach, Till I rest in peace with Thee.

REFRAIN.

Draw me nearer, nearer, blessed Lord, To the cross where Thou hast died,

nearer, nearer, nearer,

Draw me nearer, nearer, nearer, blessed Lord, To Thy precious, bleeding side.

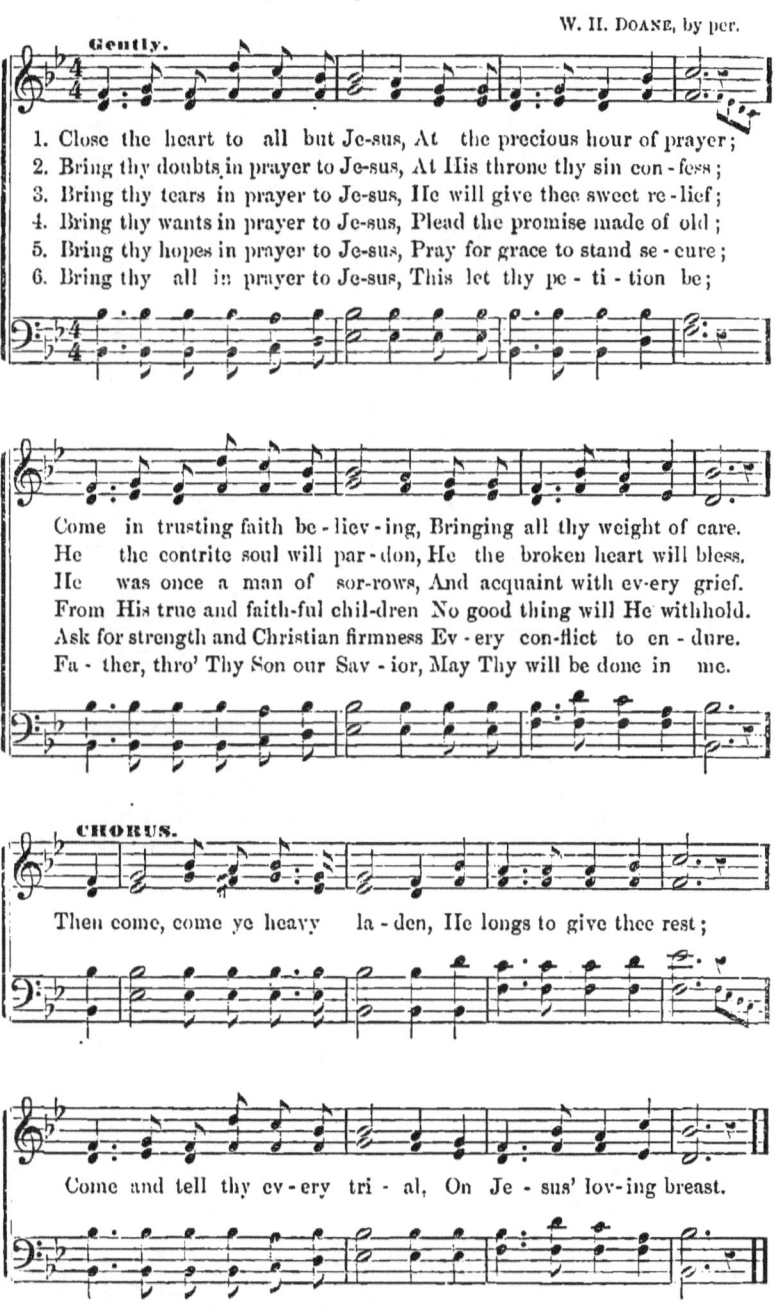

No. 36. HE IS COMING OUT TO MEET US.

"And when he was yet a great way off his father saw him, and had compassion."—Luke xv: 20.

CHESTER G. ALLEN, by per.

1. When we turn to God and leave the path of sin, When the heart repenting
2. He will guide our feet where quiet waters flow, He will lead us onward
3. At the cold dark stream of Jordan when we stand, He will bear us safe-ly

feels the need of Him; Then our gentle loving Father full of pardoning grace,
thro' the vale below; With His presence and His blessing cheer us day by day,
to the promised land; With His loving arm around us we shall hear Him say,

CHORUS.

Comes to meet us with a kind embrace.
He will come to meet us on the way. Coming out to meet us on the way,
I have come to meet you on the way.

Coming out to meet us, coming out to meet us, Oh, the joyful welcome,

see the Fa-ther now, Com-ing out to meet us on the way.

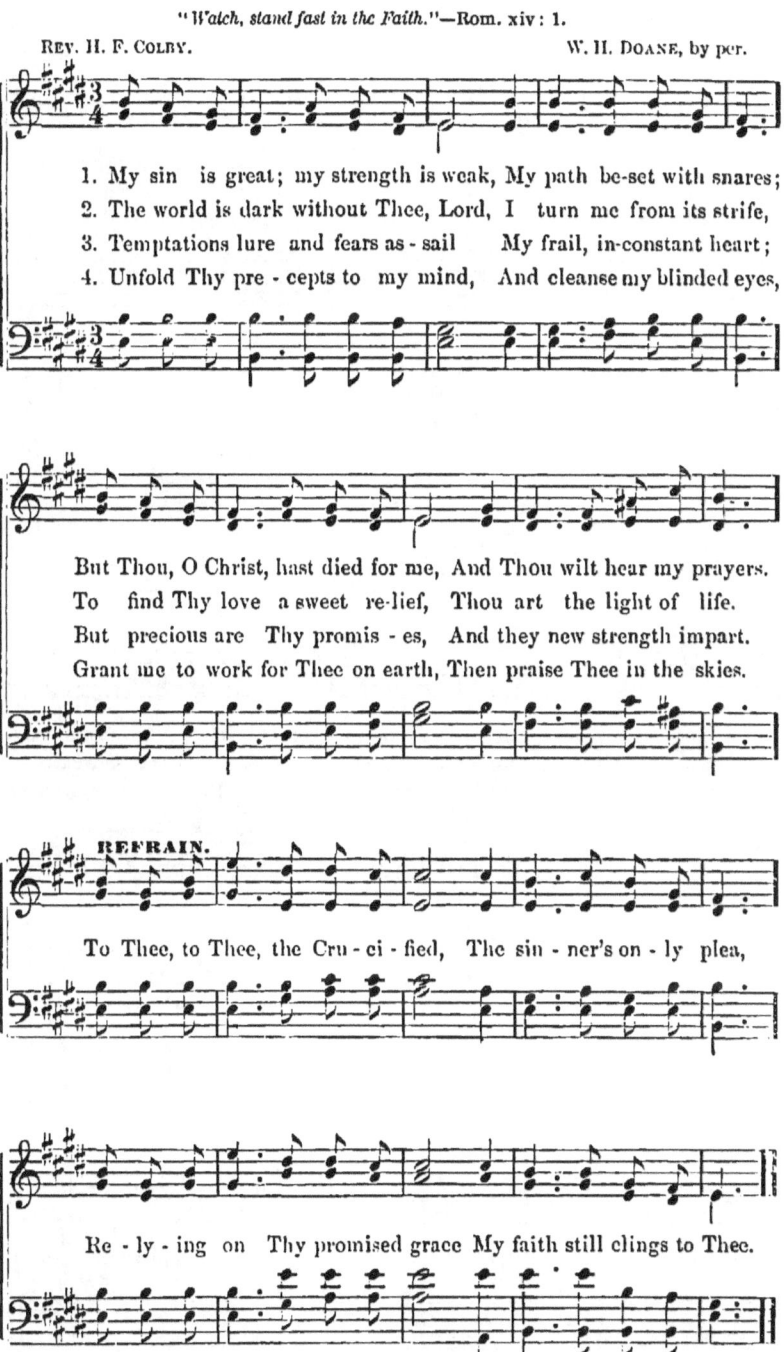

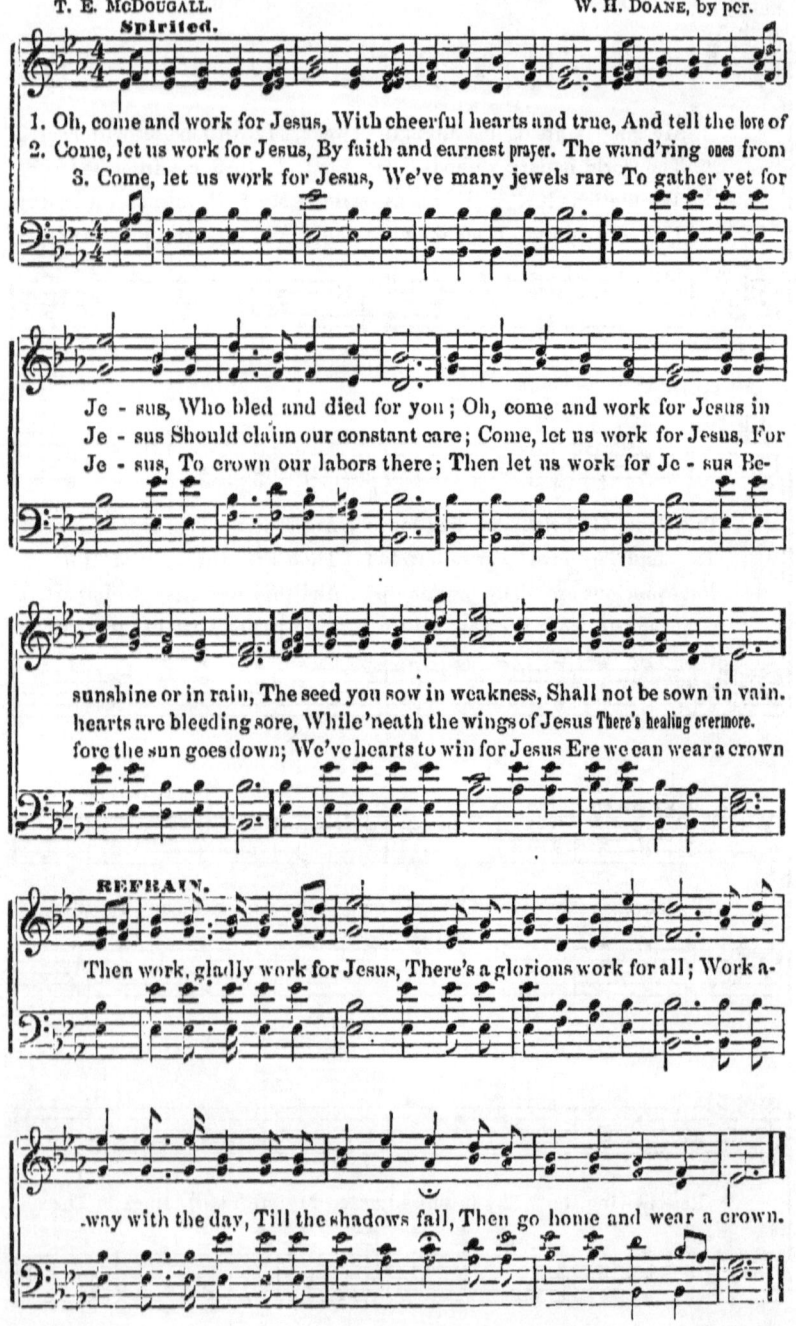

No. 41. CROWN OF LIFE.

"I will give thee a crown of life."—Rev. ii: 10.

Rev. T. L. Bailey.   R. Lowry, by per.

1. Press on, pilgrim, young tho' thou art; Firm be thy step, and brave thy heart;
2. Fight on, soldier, seek not for rest; Jesus will give when He thinks best;
3. Cheer up, Christian, for "over there" Glo-ry is beaming clear and fair;

Be-lieve the Lord, O - bey His word, And from His counsels ne'er depart.
The bat-tle o'er, To fight no more, With peace and joy thou shalt be blest.
With-in the gate The angels wait, And thine the crown the ransomed wear.

CHORUS.

Press on, pilgrim; Fight on, soldier; Cheer up, Christian; Glory thou shalt see;

To him that overcometh a crown of life shall be, And he shall reign to eternity.

The following Piece finds its Response in No. 45 (opposite page), which is intended to be sung by the Congregation, Ad Libitum.

No. 44. THOUGH YOUR SINS BE AS SCARLET.

"Though your sins be as scarlet, they shall be as white as snow."—Is. lix: 2.

W. H. Doane.

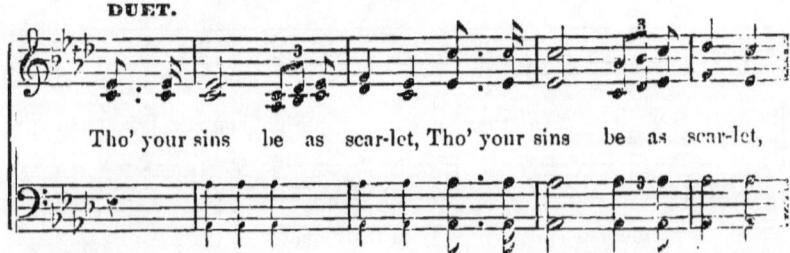

THOUGH YOUR SINS BE AS SCARLET. Concluded.

Rit.

They shall be as white as snow, They shall be as white as snow.

RESPONSE BY THE CONGREGATION.

(To No. 44.)

No. 45. JESUS I TURN TO THEE.

"Lord, to whom shall we go?"—John vi: 68.

Mrs. M. A. KIDDER. W. H. DOANE, by per.

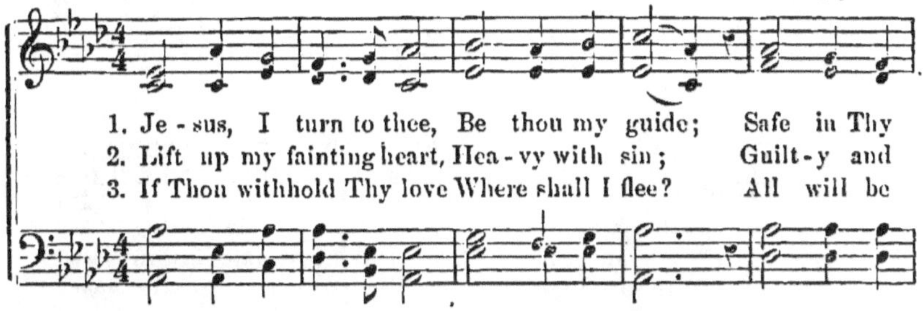

1. Je-sus, I turn to thee, Be thou my guide; Safe in Thy
2. Lift up my fainting heart, Hea-vy with sin; Guilt-y and
3. If Thou withhold Thy love Where shall I flee? All will be

lov-ing arms, There let me hide; No oth-er help I know,
full of wrong, Lord, I have been; Take me and make me white,
dark and drear, All lost to me; But, if Thy Spir-it brings

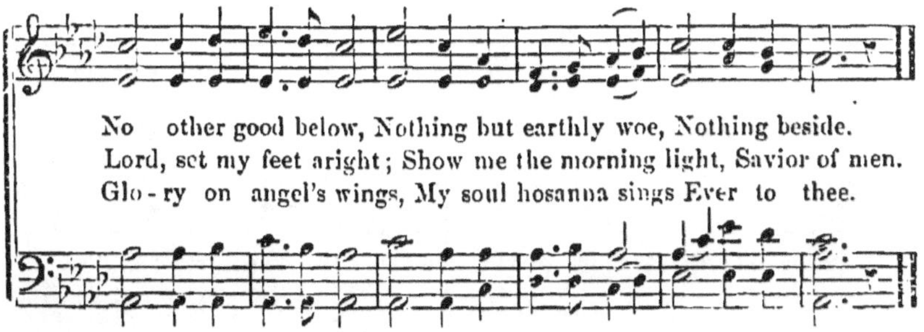

No other good below, Nothing but earthly woe, Nothing beside.
Lord, set my feet aright; Show me the morning light, Savior of men.
Glo-ry on angel's wings, My soul hosanna sings Ever to thee.

No. 46. **WHOSOEVER WILL.**

"And whosoever will, let him take the water of life freely."—Rev. xxii: 17.

Mrs. Van Alstine. W. H. Doane, by per.

1. Come a-way, O ye thirst-y, to the wa-ters; Hear the voice of the Spir-it and the Bride; They are call-ing; let ev-ery one that hear-eth Gladly seek the gen-tle flow-ing tide.

2. Come a-way, O ye dy-ing ones that lan-guish For a drop that your vig-or will re-new; Will you lin-ger and per-ish by the way-side, With the cool bright water just in view?

3. Come a-way and be re-con-ciled to Je-sus; He has died that in glo-ry you might live; He will greet you with wel-come at the foun-tain, And his blessing free-ly, free-ly give.

REFRAIN.

Who-so-ev - - er, Whoso-ev - - er, Whoso-ev-er will may come, Whoso-ev-er will may come, Freely ever will may drink the living wa-ter Free-ly flow - ing there for come and drink the fount of living water Freely flowing there for all, Freely

WHOSOEVER WILL. Concluded.

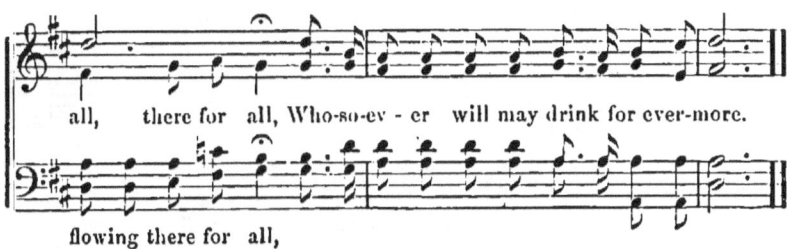

all, there for all, Who-so-ev - er will may drink for ever-more.
flowing there for all,

No. 47. THERE'LL BE JOY BY AND BY.

"Joy cometh in the morning."—Ps. xxx: 5.

Mrs. E. C. Ellsworth.   R. Lowry, by per.

1. Tho' the night be dark and dreary, Tho' the way be long and wea-ry,
2. Tho' thine eyes are sad with weeping, Thro the night thy vigils keeping,
3. Tho' thy spirit faints with fasting, Thro' the hours so slow-ly wasting,

Morn shall bring thee light and cheer; Child, look up, the dawn is near.
God shall wipe thy tears a - way, Turn thy dark - ness in - to day.
Morn shall bring a glo - rious feast, Thou shalt sit an honored guest.

CHORUS.

There'll be joy by and by, There'll be joy by and by,
In the dawning of the morning, There'll be joy by and by.

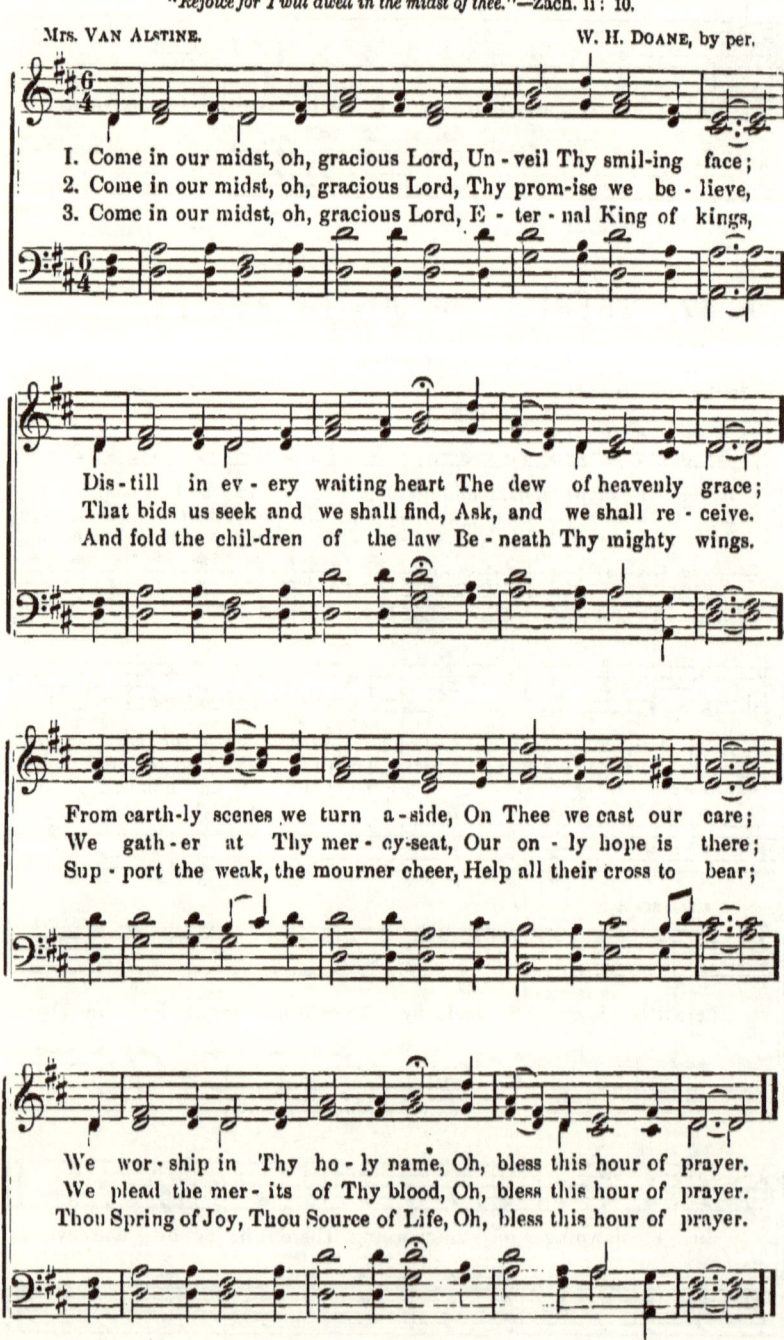

No. 51. WHAT HAST THOU DONE FOR ME?

"*So Christ was offered to bear the sins of many.*"—Heb. ix: 28.

Miss Frances R. Havergal.   W. H. Doane, by per.

1. I gave my life for thee, My precious blood I shed, That thou might'st ransom'd be,
2. I spent long years for thee, In weariness and woe, That one eternity
3. My Father's house of light, My rainbow-circled throne, I left for earthly night,
4. I suffered much for thee—More than thy tongue can tell, Of bitterest agony,
5. Oh, let thy life be given, Thy years for me bespent, World fetters all be riven,

And quickened from the dead; I gave my life for thee; What hast thou done for me?
Of joy thou mightest know; I spent long years for thee; Hast thou spent one for me?
For wand'rings sad and lone; I left it all for thee? Hast thou left aught for me?
To rescue thee from hell; I suffered much for thee; What dost thou bear for me?
And joy with suffering blent; Give thou thyself to me, And I will welcome thee.

CHORUS.

This I did for thee,   What hast thou done for me?
This I did for thee, What hast thou done for me? Yes,

This I did for thee,   What hast thou done for me?
this did for me,

No. 52. WHERE SHALL I WORK TO-DAY?

"Shew them the work that they must do."—Exod. xviii: 20.

Mrs. E. Prentiss.   W. H. Doane, by per.

Slow and gentle.

1. Hast Thou, my Master, aught for me to do To hon-or Thee to-day?
2. To which of them shall I stretch forth my hand? With sympathetic grasp,
3. But which, among them all, is mine *to-day?* Oh, guide my willing feet
4. Or unto one whose straits call not for words; To one in want, in need;

Hast Thou a word of love to some poor soul That mine may say?
Whose fainting form shall I for Thy dear sake Fond-ly en-clasp?
To some poor soul that faint-ing on the way, Needs coun-sel sweet.
Who wills not coun-sel, but would take from me A lov-ing deed.

For see, this world that Thou hast made so fair, Within its heart is sad;
Straight from my heart, each day, a blessing goes Warmly, thro' Thee, to theirs.
Or into some sick-room, where I may speak With tenderness of Thee;
Sure thou hast some work for me to do! Oh, open Thou mine eyes,

Thousands are lone-ly, thousands sigh and weep, But few are glad.
They are en-fold-ed in my in-most soul, And in my prayers.
And showing who and what Thou art, O Christ, Bid sor-row flee.
To see how thou wouldst have it done, And where it lies.

No. 53. SO NEAR TO THE KINGDOM.

"Not far from the kingdom of God."—Mark xii: 34.

F. J. C.   R. Lowry, by per.

1. So near to the kingdom! yet what dost thou lack? So near to the kingdom! what keepeth thee back? Renounce ev-ery i-dol tho' dear it may be, And come to the Sav-ior now pleading with thee.
2. So near that thou hearest the songs that resound From those who, be-liev-ing, a pardon have found! So near, yet un-will-ing to give up thy sin, When Je-sus is wait-ing to wel-come thee in!
3. Oh, come, or thy sea-son of grace will be past, The door will be closed, and this call be thy last; Oh where wouldst thou turn if the light should depart, That comes from the Spirit and shines on thy heart?
4. To die with no hope! hast thou counted the cost? To die out of Christ, and thy soul to be lost! So near to the king-dom! oh, come, we im-plore, While Je-sus is pleading, come, en-ter the door.

REFRAIN.

Plead-ing with thee, ... The Savior is pleading, is pleading with thee.
Pleading with thee, pleading with thee,

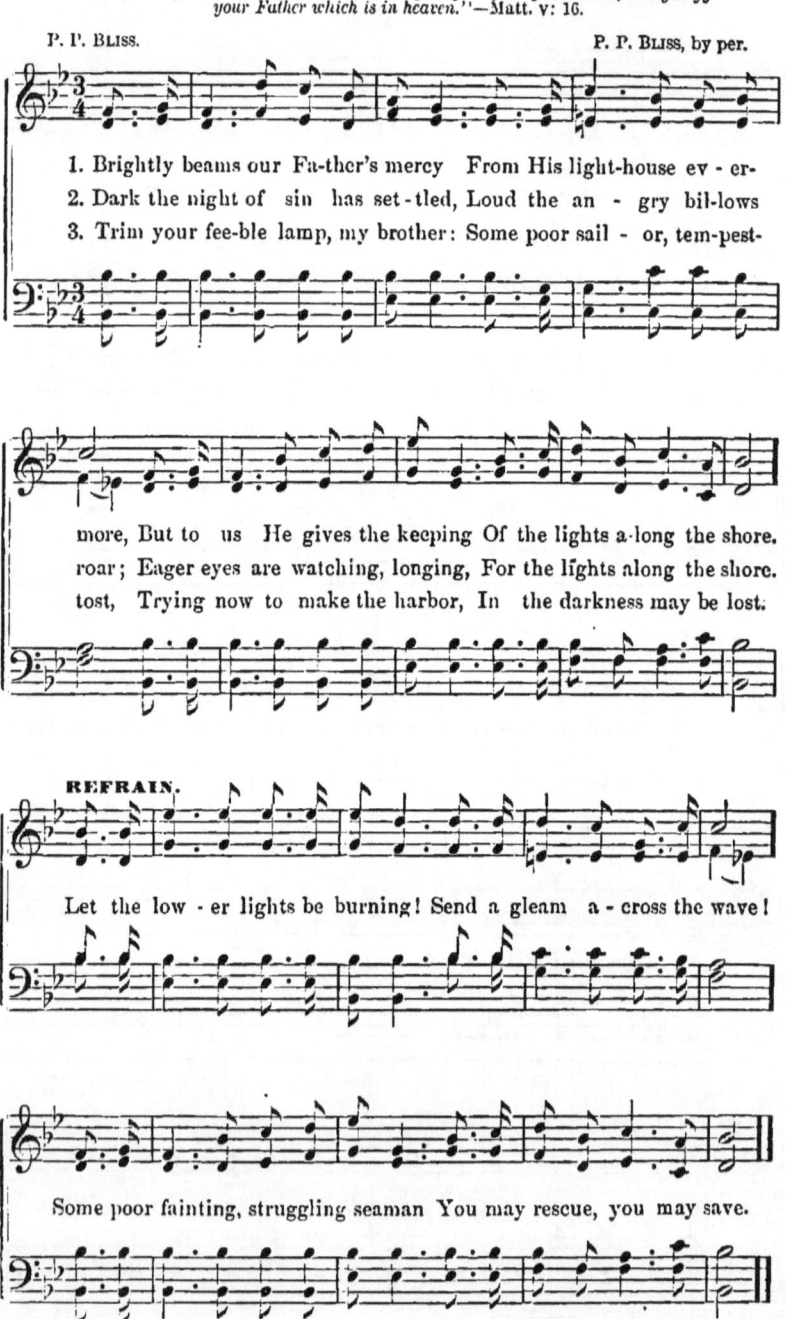

No. 57. HOLD IT UP TO THE WORLD.

"Go ye into all the world and preach the gospel to every creature."—Mark xvi: 15.

W. H. DOANE, by per.

1. Take the cross, take the cross, hold it up to the world, With its banner of hope by the Savior unfurled; Hold it up, and the lost to its refuge may flee Where the dear Savior pleads: I am seeking for thee.
2. Lift it high, lift it high, let the friendless be-hold; There are hearts that will weep when its story is told; Lift it high, and the poor to its shelter may flee Where the dear Savior pleads: I have suffered for thee.
3. Take the cross, take the cross, and re-joice in the Lord; Go ye forth, go ye forth in the strength of His word; Hold it up, and the eye of the careless may see Where the dear Savior pleads: I was wounded for thee.
4. Oh, the cross, bless-ed cross, with the blood crimson tide Like a river of love flowing down from its side; To the cross all may come; hold it up and proclaim Here is pardon and peace thro' a Savior's dear name,

REFRAIN.

Hold it up to the world, Hold it up to the world;
Hold it upward, hold it upward, Hold it upward, hold it upward,
Fal-ter nev-er, hold it ev-er, Hold it up to the world.

No. 58. I NEED THEE EVERY HOUR.

"Without me ye can do nothing."—John xv: 5.

Mrs. A. S. Hawks. R. Lowry, by per.

1. I need Thee every hour, Most gracious Lord; No tender voice like thine
2. I need Thee every hour; Stay Thou near by; Temptations lose their pow'r
3. I need Thee every hour, In joy or pain; Come quickly and a-bide,
4. I need Thee every hour; Teach me Thy will; And Thy rich promises
5. I need Thee every hour, Most Holy One; Oh, make me Thine indeed,

REFRAIN.

Can peace af-ford.
When Thou art nigh.   I need Thee, oh! I need Thee; Every hour I
Or life is vain.
In me ful-fill.
Thou bless-ed Son.

need Thee; Oh, bless me now, my Sav-ior! I come to Thee!

No. 59. JESUS WAITS FOR THEE.

"Come unto me."—Isa. lv: 3.

Rev. Geo. B. Peck. Hubert P. Main, by per..

Tenderly.

1. Come, come to Je-sus! He waits to wel-come thee,
2. Come, come to Je-sus! He waits to ran-som thee,
3. Come, come to Je-sus! He waits to light-en thee,
4. Come, come to Je-sus! He waits to give to thee,

JESUS WAITS FOR THEE. Concluded.

O Wand'rer, ea - ger - ly; Come, come to Je - sus!
O Slave, e - ter - nal - ly; Come, come to Je - sus!
O Bur-dened! gra - cious-ly; Come, come to Je - sus!
O Blind! a vi - sion free! Come, come to Je - sus!

5 Come, come to Jesus!
He waits to shelter thee,
O Weary! blessedly;
Come, come to Jesus!

6 Come, come to Jesus!
He waits to carry thee,
O Lamb! so lovingly;
Come, come to Jesus!

No. 60. MORE FAITHFUL TO THEE.

"Be ye holy."—Lev. xx: 7.

F. J. C.   W. H. DOANE, by per.

Slow.

1. Draw nearer, my Savior, In mer-cy be - hold, And keep me for-ev-er Safe, safe in the fold; More watchful and trusting, Oh, help me to be, More ho-ly, dear Savior, More faithful to Thee.
2. More humble in spir-it, More fervent in pray'r, More cheerful and willing My tri - als to bear; More ear-nest in la - bor,
3. Come, blessed Redeemer, Now dwell in my heart, My hope and my comfort, For ev - er Thou art; In all my tempta - tions,

No. 61. LORD, AT THY MERCY-SEAT.

"I will commune with thee from above."—Num. vii: 89.

F. J. CROSBY.

1. Lord, at Thy mer-cy-seat, Hum-bly I fall; Pleading Thy prom-ise sweet, Lord, hear my call. Now let Thy work be-gin, Oh, make me pure within, Cleanse me from every sin, Je-sus, my all.
2. Tears of re-pentant grief Si-lent-ly fall; Help Thou my un-be-lief, Hear Thou my call. Oh, how I pine for Thee, 'Tis all my hope, my plea, Je-sus has died for me, Je-sus, my all.
3. Hark! how the words of love Ten-der-ly fall; Ere to the realms a-bove, Heard is my call. Now ev-ery doubt has flown, Broken my heart of stone, Lord, I am Thine alone, Je-sus, my all.
4. Still at Thy mer-cy-seat, Hum-bly I fall; Pleading Thy prom-ise sweet, Heard is my call. Faith wings my soul to Thee, This all my hope shall be, Je-sus has died for me, Je-sus, my all.

No. 62. OVER THE OCEAN WAVE. Missionary.

"I will give thee the heathen for thine inheritance."—Psa. ii: 8.

Arr. by W. H. D.

1. O-ver the ocean wave, Far, far a-way, There the poor heathen live,
2. Here in this happy land we have the light Shining from God's own word,
3. Then, while the mission ships glad tidings bring, List! as that heathen land

CHOR. Pit-y them, pit-y them, Christians at home, Haste with the bread of life,

OVER THE OCEAN WAVE. Concluded.

D. C. CHORUS.

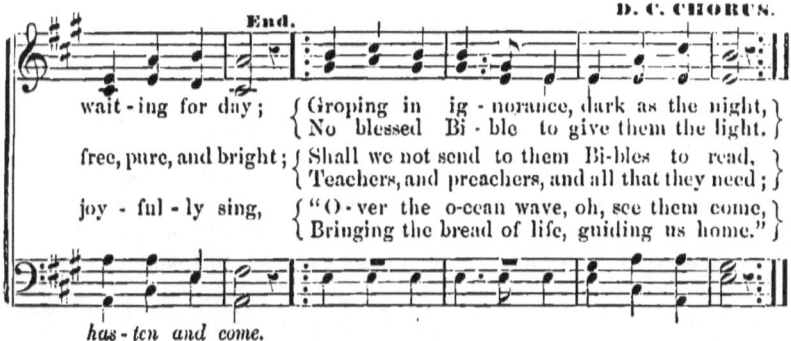

wait - ing for day; { Groping in ig - norance, dark as the night, No blessed Bi - ble to give them the light. }
free, pure, and bright; { Shall we not send to them Bi - bles to read, Teachers, and preachers, and all that they need; }
joy - ful - ly sing, { "O - ver the o-cean wave, oh, see them come, Bringing the bread of life, guiding us home." }

has - ten and come.

No. 63. IN THE VALLEY. Quartette.

"*They seek a country.*"—Heb. xi : 14.

Mrs. ANNIE S. HAWKS.　　　　　　　　　　　　　　　R. LOWRY, by per.

Slow.

1. A few more prayers—a few more tears—It wont be long, it wont be
2. A lit - tle pain—a lit - tle joy—And, less or more, it mat-ters
3. A lit - tle gathering of the loved, Whose patient hearts were always
4. But Jesus' love—His precious love—Will be my stay—my on - ly

long,—A few more months, a few more years, Will hush my song—this earthly
not; Some mingling yet with earth's alloy, And then forgot—ah! soon for-
true; Some tears to mingle with the sod—A ver - y few—a ver-y
stay; And radiance, gleaming from above, Will light the way—the lonely

song; And then I shall sleep, (I shall sleep) in the val - ley.
got— While I sleep, calm-ly sleep, (calmly sleep) in the val - ley.
few— When they lay me to rest, (me to rest) in the val - ley.
way— When my soul pass-es thro', (pass-es thro') the dark val - ley.

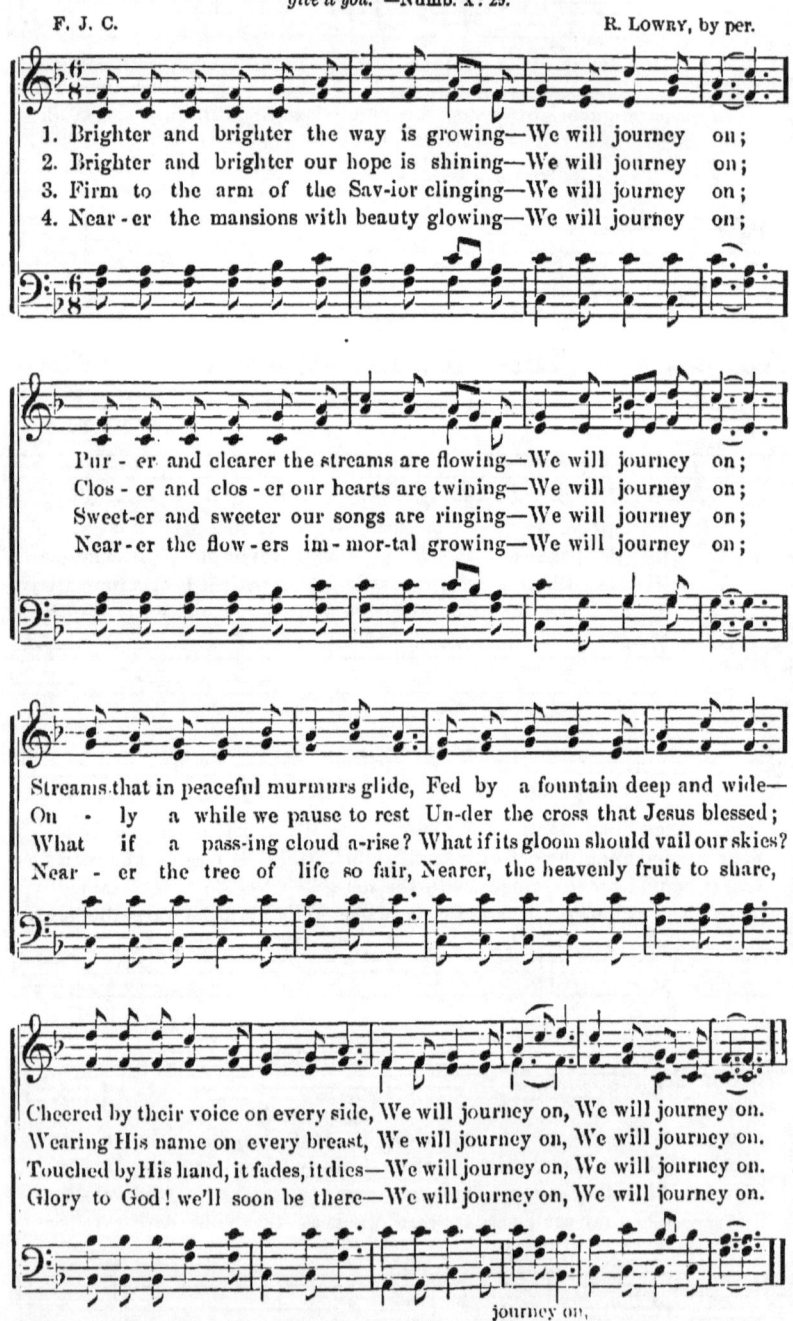

No. 65. TELL IT WITH JOY.

"*My brethren, rejoice in the Lord.*"—Phil. iii: 1.

F. J. CROSBY.   W. H. DOANE, by per.

1. Tell it with joy, Tell it with joy; Love in my bos-om is glowing;
2. Tell it with joy, Tell it with joy; Wonder-ful, won-der-ful sto-ry!
3. Come unto Him, Come unto Him; Mer-cy is ten-der-ly pleading;

REFRAIN.

Jesus' blood has cleansed me, Jesus has made me free: 1. Tell it again,
I was lost till mer-cy Gently came down from heav'n: 2,3. Tell it with joy,
Wea-ry, hea-vy la-den, Still there is room for thee: On-ly believe,

Tell it a-gain; Oh, the sweet rapture of par-don! Grace divine has
Tell it with joy; Now I am hap-py in Je-sus; All is calm and
On-ly believe; Je-sus is ready and willing; All may come and

End.

saved me, And Je-sus my all shall be.   Wea-ry and lone-ly,
peace-ful, And all of my sins for-given.   I will a-dore Him,
wel-come, Sal-va-tion for all is free.   Why will ye lin-ger?

D. S.

Seeking in vain for pleasure, Far from the fold my spirit had gone astray:
Je-sus, my dear Redeemer, Yes I will give Him glory from day to day.
Mer-cy is still entreating, Come and be happy, come and with rapture say—

6

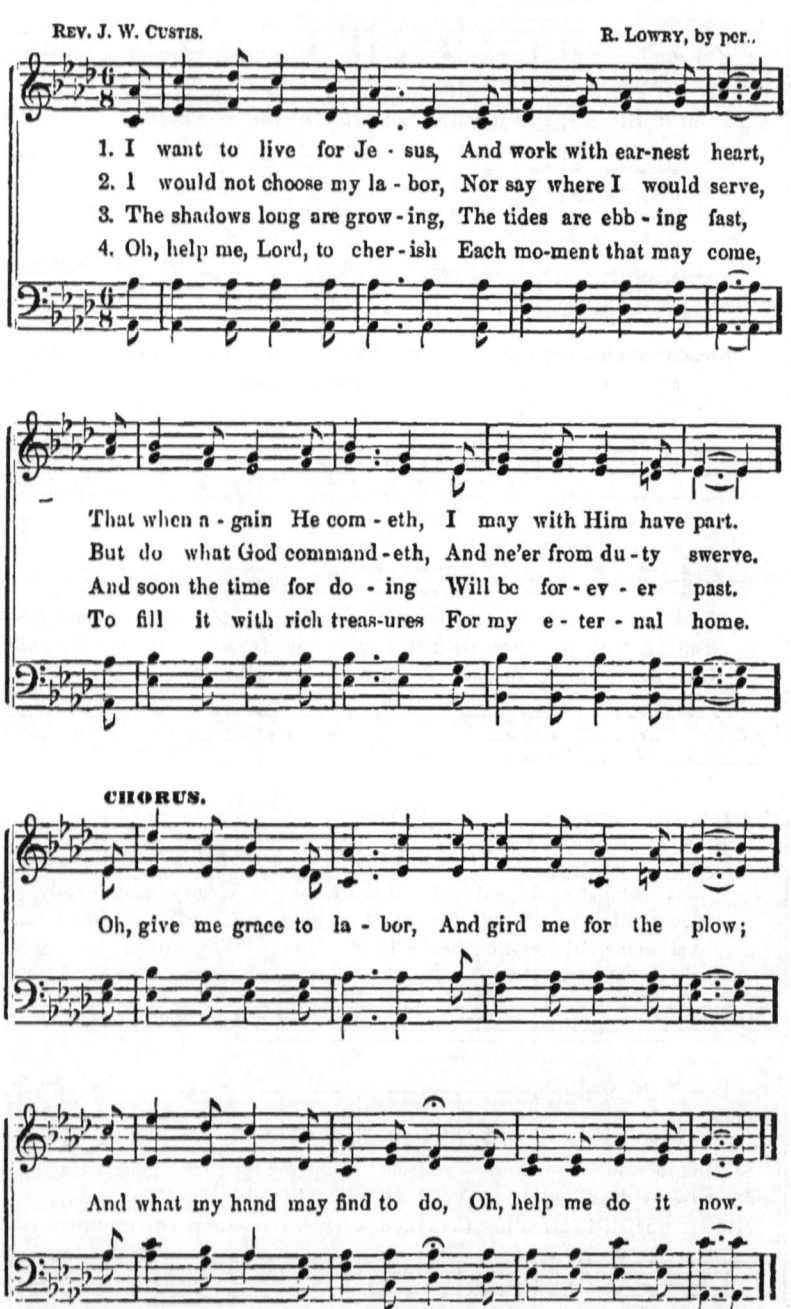

No. 67. MORE LIKE JESUS.

"*We shall be like him.*"—1 John iii: 2.

FANNY CROSBY.   W. H. DOANE, by per.

Slow, with feeling.

1. More like Je-sus would I be, Let my Sav-ior dwell with me;
2. If He hears the ra-ven's cry, If His ev-er-watchful eye
3. More like Je-sus when I pray, More like Je-sus day by day,

Fill my soul with peace and love—Make me gentle as a dove;
Marks the sparrows when they fall, Sure-ly He will hear my call.
May I rest me by His side, Where the tranquil wa-ters glide.

More like Je-sus while I go, Pil-grim in this world be-low;
He will teach me how to live, All my simple thoughts forgive;
Born of Him through grace renewed, By His love my will sub-dued,

Poor in spir-it would I be, Let my Savior dwell in me.
Pure in heart I still would be— Let my Savior dwell in me.
Rich in faith I still would be— Let my Savior dwell in me.

No. 68. THE LOST SHEEP.

"Go after that which is lost."—Luke xv: 4.

F. J. C. W. H. DOANE, by per.

1. From the hundred sheep which the Shepherd's care Had protected many a day, There was one went forth, and its rest-less feet In the desert wandered away; Then the Shepherd's heart was grieved, and He kind-ly said: On the mountain it will languish and pine; I will go and search for the sheep I lost, I will leave the ninety and nine.

2. There was joy, great joy in the Shepherd's fold, When His long, long journey was o'er, And the poor lost sheep that had gone a-stray, In His arms He tenderly bore; Then the Shepherd's heart was glad, and He said to all: What a moment of re-joic-ing is mine! For I love my sheep that I lost and found, More than all the ninety and nine.

3. Oh, that Shepherd kind is the Son of God, Who has borne our sorrow and care; It was He who said there is joy in heaven O'er the wanderer's penitent prayer; To the soul He bringeth back to His fold of grace, To His precious fold of mer-cy di-vine, How His heart goes out, for He loves that one More than all the ninety and nine.

No. 69. THE PRODIGAL CHILD.

"I will arise and go to my father."—Luke xv: 18.

Mrs. E. H. Gates. W. H. Doane, by per.

Slow, with feeling.

1. Come home, come home, You are weary at heart, For the way has been dark, And so lonely and wild. O Prodigal Child! Come
2. Come home, come home, For we watch and we wait, And we stand at the gate, While the shadows are piled. O Prodigal Child! Come
3. Come home, come home, From the sorrow and blame, From the sin and the shame, And the tempter that smiled. O Prodigal Child! Come
4. Come home, come home, There is bread and to spare, And a warm welcome there, Then, to friends reconciled, O Prodigal Child! Come

CHORUS. Rit.

home, oh, come home! Come home, Come, oh, come home, Come home,
Come home, come home,

No. 70. TO-DAY THE SAVIOR CALLS. (Amoy).

"To-day if ye will hear his voice."—Ps. xcv. 7.

Dr. L. Mason, by per.

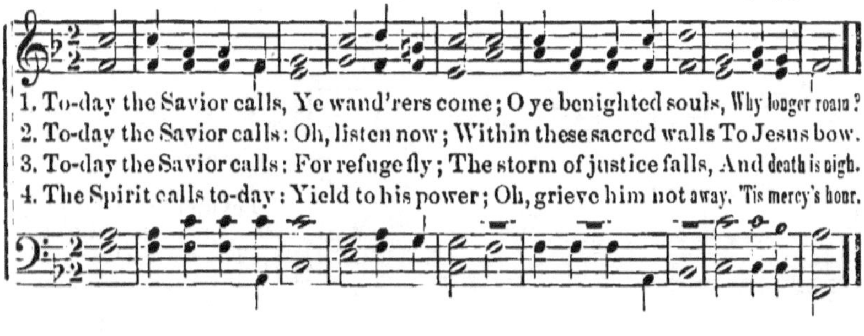

1. To-day the Savior calls, Ye wand'rers come; O ye benighted souls, Why longer roam?
2. To-day the Savior calls: Oh, listen now; Within these sacred walls To Jesus bow.
3. To-day the Savior calls: For refuge fly; The storm of justice falls, And death is nigh.
4. The Spirit calls to-day: Yield to his power; Oh, grieve him not away, 'Tis mercy's hour.

No. 73.   OH, TO BE NOTHING.

"Neither is he that planteth anything, neither he that watereth."—1 Cor. iii : 7.

GEORGIANA M. TAYLOR, 1869.   R. GEO. HALLS, by per. Arr. by P. P. BLISS.

Very slow.

1. Oh, to be noth-ing, noth-ing, On-ly to lie at His feet,
2. Oh, to be noth-ing, noth-ing, On-ly as led by His hand;
3. Oh, to be noth-ing, noth-ing, Painful the humbling may be,

CHO. Oh, to be noth-ing, noth-ing, On-ly to lie at His feet,

FINE.

A brok-en and emptied ves-sel, For the Master's use made meet.
A mes-senger at His gate-way, On-ly waiting for His command.
Yet low in the dust I'd lay me, That the world might my Savior see.

A bro-ken and emp-tied ves-sel, For the Mas-ter's use made meet.

Emptied that He might fill me As forth to His serv-ice I go;
On-ly an instrument read-y His praises to sound at His will,
Rather be noth-ing, noth-ing, To Him let their voices be raised,

D. C. CHORUS.

Broken, that so un-hin-dered, His life through me might flow.
Willing, should He not require me, In silence to wait on Him still.
He is the Fountain of bless-ing, He on-ly is meet to be praised.

No. 74. NEAR THE CROSS.

"Peace through the blood of his cross."—Coll. 1: 29.

FANNY J. CROSBY. W. H. DOANE, by per.

1. Je - sus, keep me near the cross, There a pre - cious fountain
2. Near the cross, a trembling soul, Love and mer - cy found me;
3. Near the cross, O Lamb of God, Bring its scenes be - fore me;
4. Near the cross I'll watch and wait, Hop - ing, trust - ing ev - er,

Free to all— a heal-ing stream, Flows from Calvary's mountain.
There the bright and morning star Shed its beams a-round me.
Help me walk from day to day, With its shadows o'er me.
Till I reach the gold - en strand, Just be - yond the riv - er.

REFRAIN.

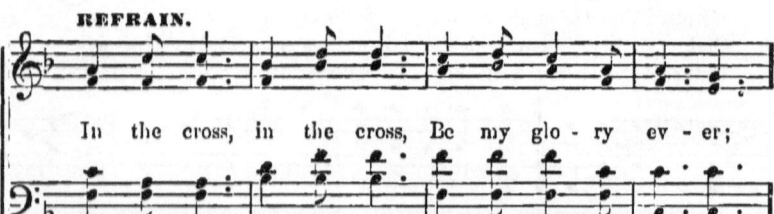

In the cross, in the cross, Be my glo - ry ev - er;

Till my raptured soul shall find Rest be - yond the riv - er.

No. 75. WEARY ONE, WAND'RING ONE.

"Speak a word in season to him that is weary."—Isa. 1: 4.

R. Geo. Hall. Arr. by W. H. Doane.

Weary one, wand'ring one, Jesus is calling thee; Weary one, wand'ring one, calling thee home.

1. Hard hath He fought for thee, Tender-ly sought for thee, See, He has brought for thee Par-don at home.
2. Come, for the Sav-ior's face Mak-eth each des-ert place Shining with love and peace All the way home.
3. No foe shall en-ter there, No bur-den en-ter there, Je-sus, the cen-ter there, Call-eth the home.

REFRAIN.

Wea-ry one, wand'ring one, Je-sus is call-ing thee, Je-sus is call-ing thee, List-en and come.

No. 76. MORE LOVE TO THEE, O CHRIST.

"Continue ye in my love."—John xv: 19.

Mrs. E. PRENTISS. W. H. DOANE, by per.

1. More love to thee, O Christ! More love to thee! Hear thou the prayer I make, On bended knee; This is my earnest plea; More love, O Christ, to Thee, More love to Thee, More love to Thee.
2. Once earthly joy I craved, Sought peace and rest, Now Thee alone I seek, Give what is best: This all my prayer shall be;
3. Let sorrow do its work, Send grief and pain, Sweet are Thy messengers, Sweet their refrain, When they can sing with me—
4. Then shall my latest breath Whisper Thy praise; This be the parting cry My heart shall raise, This still its prayer shall be:

No. 77. THERE IS NONE LIKE JESUS.

"Cast your care on Him, for he careth for you."—1 Pet. v: 7.

R. LOWRY, by per.

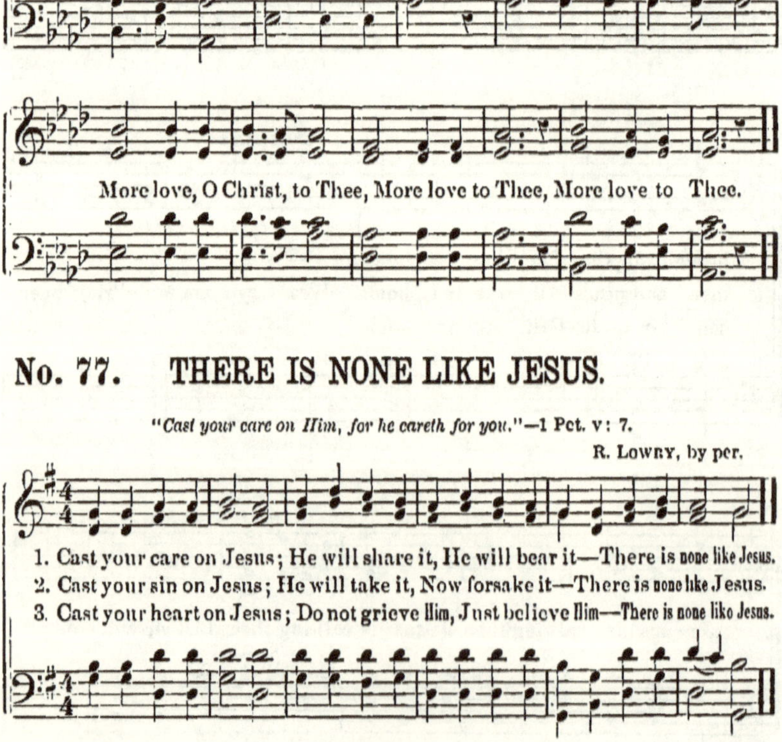

1. Cast your care on Jesus; He will share it, He will bear it—There is none like Jesus.
2. Cast your sin on Jesus; He will take it, Now forsake it—There is none like Jesus.
3. Cast your heart on Jesus; Do not grieve Him, Just believe Him—There is none like Jesus.

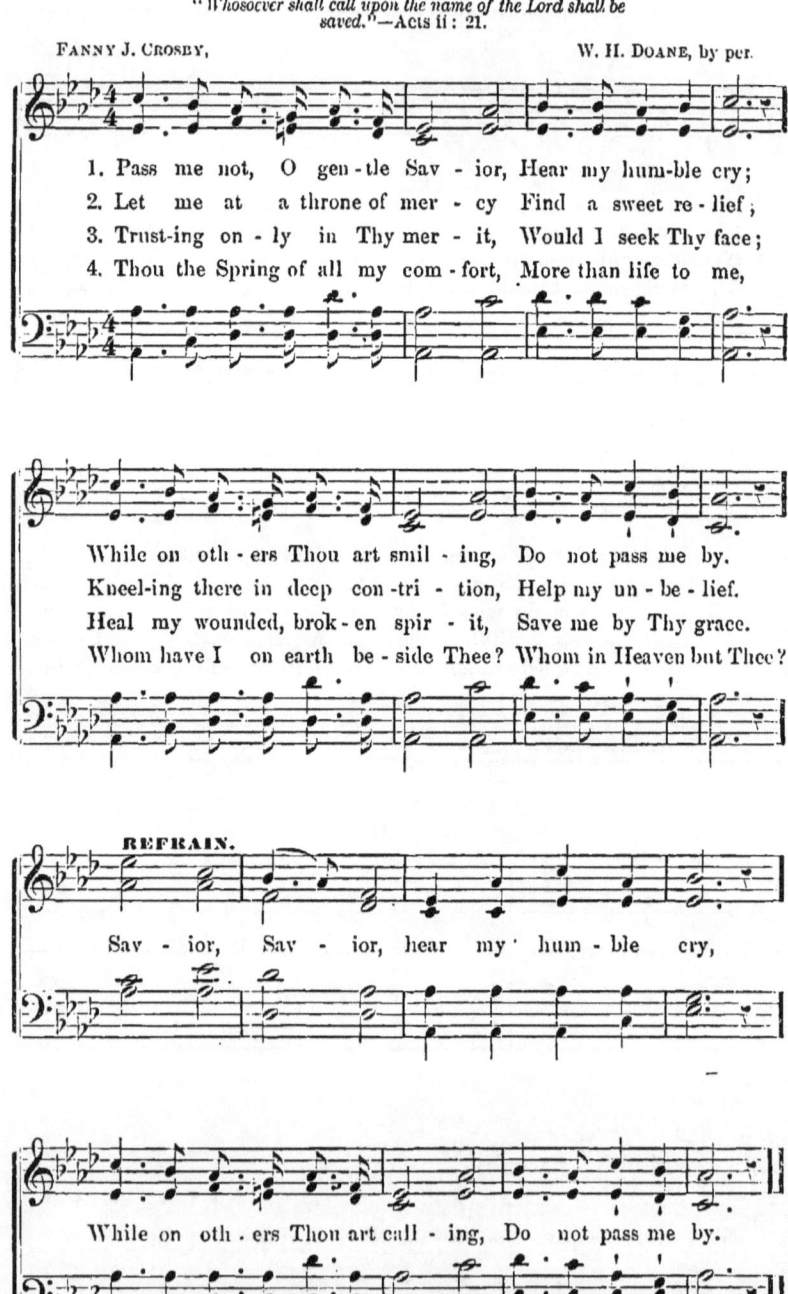

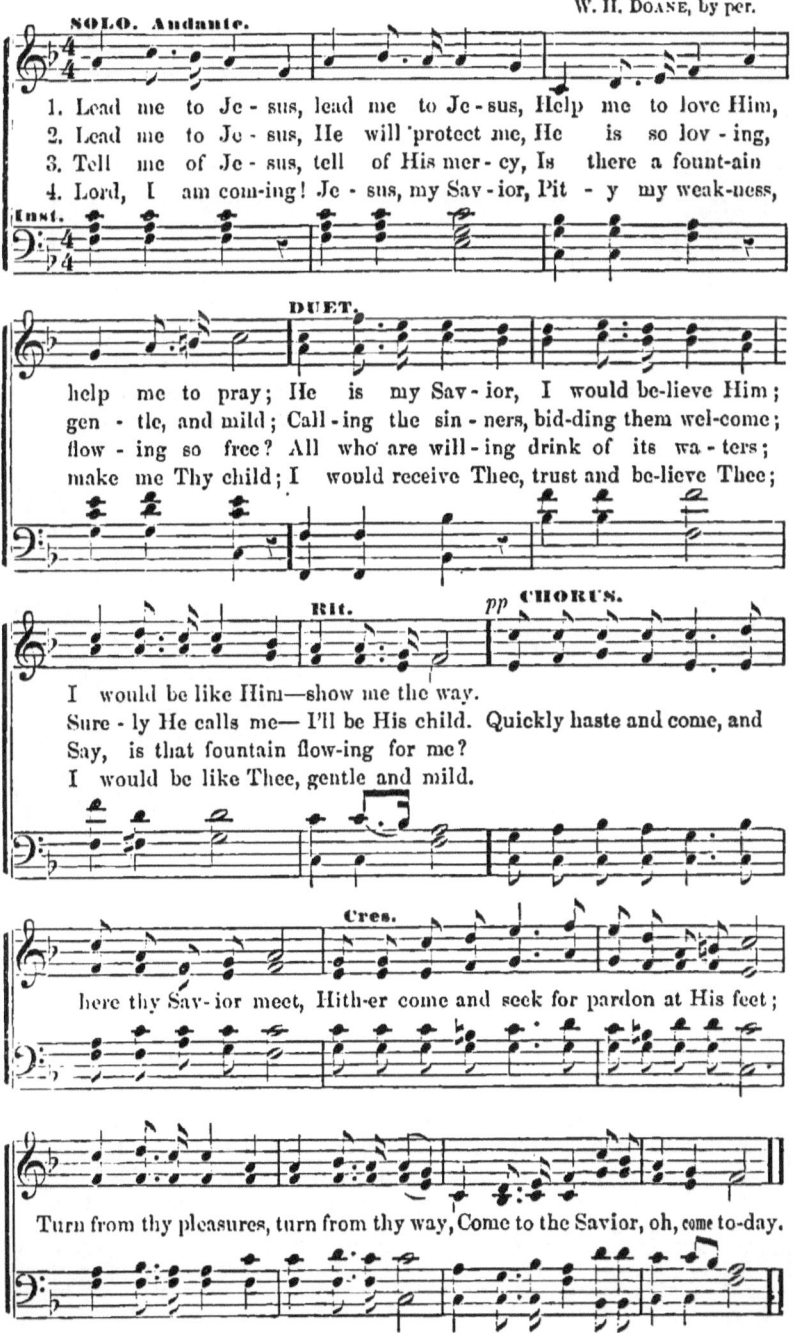

No. 80. LEAD ME TO JESUS.

"He went about seeking some to lead him."—Acts xiii: 11.

W. H. Doane, by per.

1. Lead me to Jesus, lead me to Jesus, Help me to love Him, help me to pray; He is my Savior, I would believe Him; I would be like Him—show me the way.
2. Lead me to Jesus, He will protect me, He is so loving, gentle, and mild; Calling the sinners, bidding them welcome; Surely He calls me— I'll be His child.
3. Tell me of Jesus, tell of His mercy, Is there a fountain flowing so free? All who are willing drink of its waters; Say, is that fountain flowing for me?
4. Lord, I am coming! Jesus, my Savior, Pity my weakness, make me Thy child; I would receive Thee, trust and believe Thee; I would be like Thee, gentle and mild.

CHORUS.

Quickly haste and come, and here thy Savior meet, Hither come and seek for pardon at His feet; Turn from thy pleasures, turn from thy way, Come to the Savior, oh, come to-day.

No. 81. SAVIOR, WE WAIT FOR THEE.

"Our soul waiteth for the Lord."—Psa. xxxii: 20.

Mrs. M. A. KIDDER.   W. H. D.

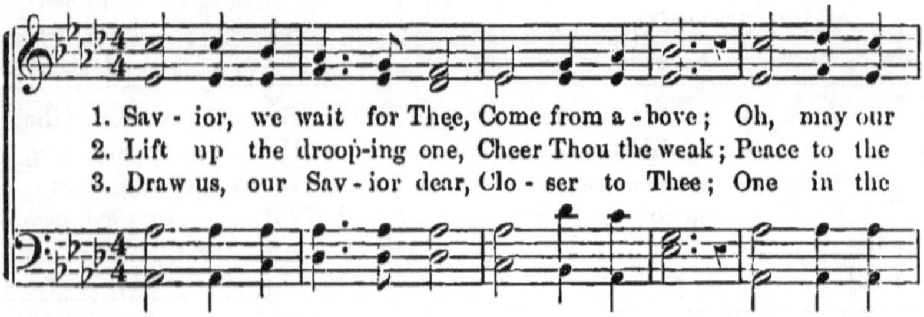

1. Sav-ior, we wait for Thee, Come from a-bove; Oh, may our grate-ful hearts Burn with Thy love. Here in com-mun-ion sweet, Here, at Thy mercy-seat, Je-sus, Thy children meet, Come from above.
2. Lift up the droop-ing one, Cheer Thou the weak; Peace to the mourn-ing soul Ten-der-ly speak. Guide Thou our thoughts aright, Grant us Thy holy light, Oh, make our path more bright, While Thee we seek.
3. Draw us, our Sav-ior dear, Clo-ser to Thee; One in the bonds of love Help us to be. Then when life's storms are o'er, On yonder radiant shore, We'll meet to part no more, Happy in Thee.

No. 82. I LOVE THEE.

"Thou knowest that I love thee."—John xxi: 17.

Mrs. ANNIE S. HAWKS.   R. LOWRY, by per.

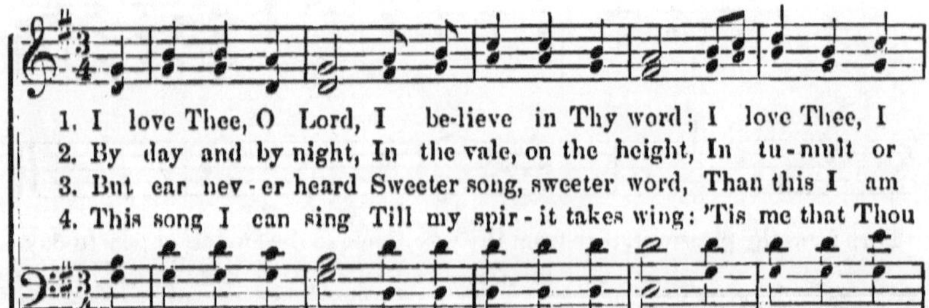

1. I love Thee, O Lord, I be-lieve in Thy word; I love Thee, I
2. By day and by night, In the vale, on the height, In tu-mult or
3. But ear nev-er heard Sweeter song, sweeter word, Than this I am
4. This song I can sing Till my spir-it takes wing; 'Tis me that Thou

I LOVE THEE. Concluded.

REFRAIN.

love Thee, I love Thee, my Lord.
si - lence, Thou art my de - light. How sweet to love Thee—In Thy
sing - ing: Thou lov-est me, Lord.
lov - est, My Sav-ior and King.

pres-ence to be! But sweeter, far sweeter, That Thou lovest me.

No. 83. ALAS! AND DID MY SAVIOR BLEED?

"He was bruised for our iniquities."—Isa. liii: 5.

ISAAC WATTS, 1709.   W. H. D.

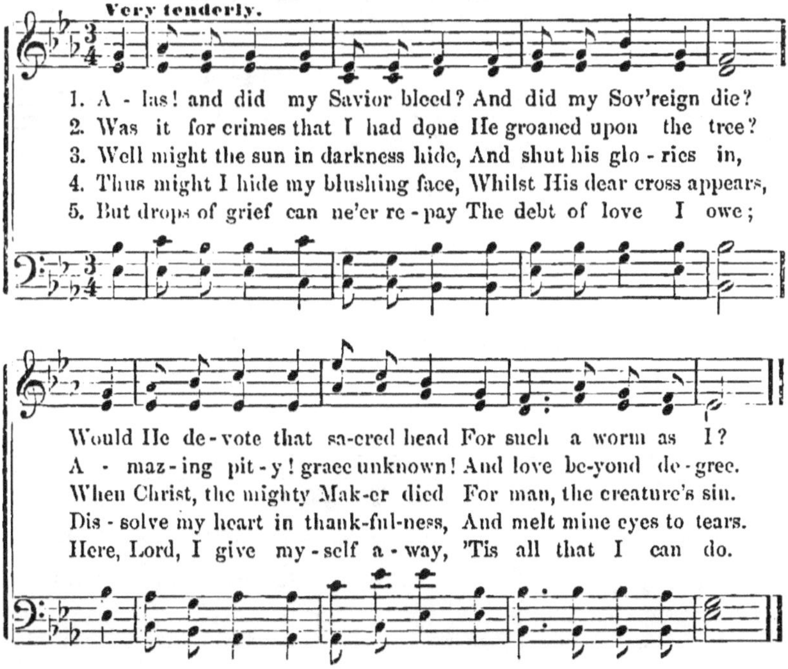

Very tenderly.

1. A - las! and did my Savior bleed? And did my Sov'reign die?
2. Was it for crimes that I had done He groaned upon the tree?
3. Well might the sun in darkness hide, And shut his glo - ries in,
4. Thus might I hide my blushing face, Whilst His dear cross appears,
5. But drops of grief can ne'er re - pay The debt of love I owe;

Would He de - vote that sa-cred head For such a worm as I?
A - maz-ing pit - y! grace unknown! And love be-yond de - gree.
When Christ, the mighty Mak-er died For man, the creature's sin.
Dis - solve my heart in thank-ful-ness, And melt mine eyes to tears.
Here, Lord, I give my-self a - way, 'Tis all that I can do.

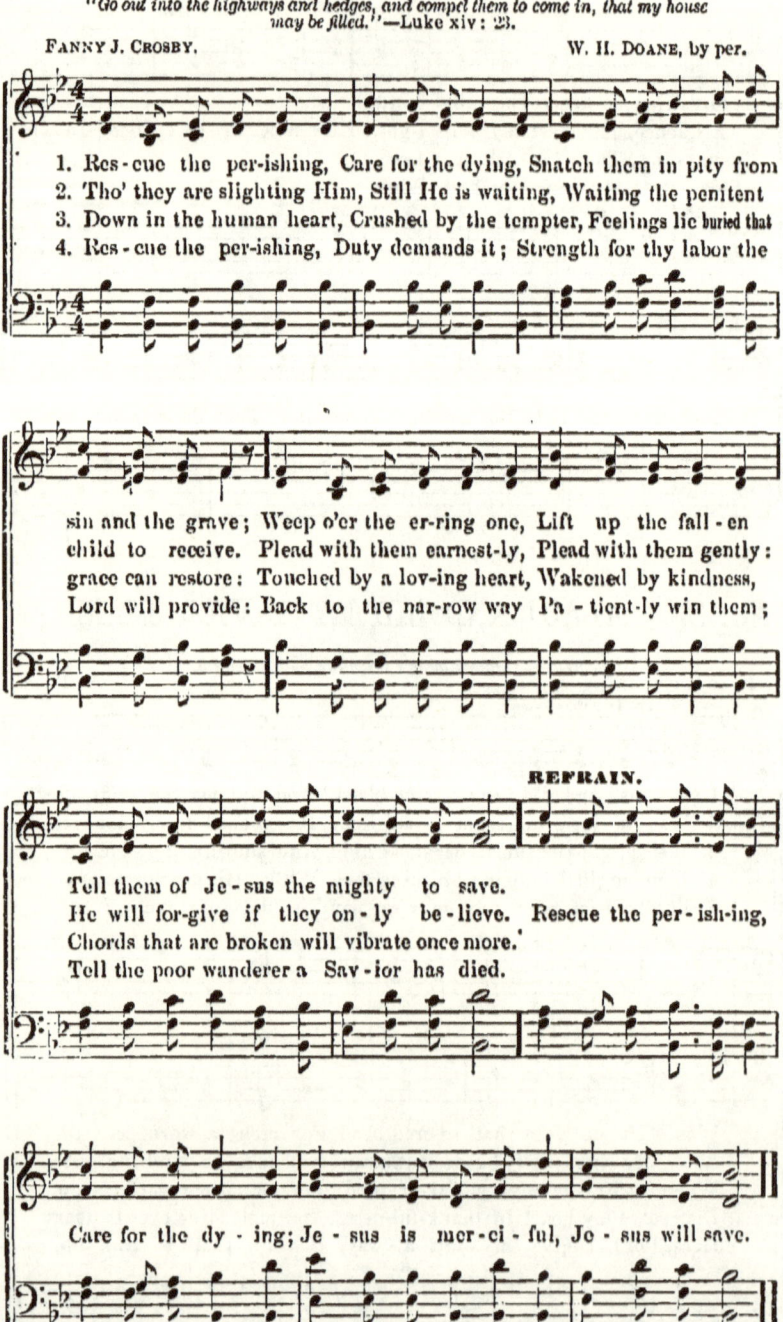

No. 85. HALLELUJAH! WHO SHALL PART?

"Who shall separate us from the love of Christ?"—Rom. viii: 35.

WM. DICKINSON.   R. LOWRY, by per.

1. Hallelujah! who shall part Christ's own church from Christ's own heart? Sever from the Sav-ior's side Souls for whom the Sav-ior died? Dash one precious jewel down From Immanuel's blood-bright crown.
2. Hallelujah? shall the sword Part us from our glorious Lord? Trouble dark or dire dis-grace E'er the Spirit's seal ef - face? Fam-ine, na-ked-ness, or hate Bride and bridegroom separate.

3 Hallelujah! life nor death,
Powers above nor powers beneath,
Monarch's might nor tyrant's doom,
Things that are nor things to come,
Men nor angels, e'er shall part
Christ's own church from Christ's own heart.

No. 86. KEEP ME, LORD, FOREVER THINE.

"And I will put my Spirit within you."—Ezek. xxxvi: 27.

JOHN STOCKER, 1776.   Arr. from English by W. H. D.
Gently.   FINE.

1. Gra-cious Spir - it, love di-vine, Let Thy light with-in me shine;
   All my guilt - y fears re-move, Fill me full of heaven and love.
2. Life and peace to me im-part, Seal sal - va - tion on my heart;
   Breathe Thyself in - to my breast, Ear-nest of im-mor-tal rest.
3. Let me nev-er from Thee stray, Keep me in the nar-row way;
   Fill my soul with joy di - vine, Keep me, Lord, for - ev - er Thine.

REF. Keep me, Lord, for - ev - er Thine, Let Thy light with - in me shine.

D.C. Refrain.

No. 87. WAITING AND WATCHING FOR ME.

"*I shall go to him * * * he shall not return to me.*"—2 Sam. xii: 23.

ANON.   P. P. BLISS, by per.

Slowly.

1. When my fin - al fare-well to the world I have said, And gladly lie down
2. There are lit - tle ones glancing a-bout in my path, In want of a friend
3. There are old and forsaken who linger awhile In homes which their dear-
4. Oh, should I be brought there by the bountiful grace Of Him who delights

to my rest; When softly the watchers shall say, "He is dead," And
and a guide; There are dear little eyes looking up into mine, Whose
est have left; And a few gen - tle words or an ac-tion of love May
to for - give, Though I bless not the weary about in my path, Pray

fold my pale hands o'er my breast; And when, with my glo - ri - fied
tears might be eas - i - ly dried. But Je - sus may beck-on the
cheer their sad spirits be - reft. But the Reaper is near to the
on - ly for self while I live,— Methinks I should mourn o'er my

vis - ion at last The walls of "That Cit - y" I see.
chil-dren a - way In the midst of their grief and their glee—
long stand-ing corn, The wea - ry will soon be set free—
sin - ful neg - lect, If sor - row in heav - en can be,

1-3. Will any one then at the beauti - ful gate, Be waiting and watching for
4. Should no one I love at the beautiful gate, Be waiting and watching for

me? Will an - y one then, at the beau - ti - ful gate, Be
me! Should no one I love at the beau - ti - ful gate, Be

WAITING AND WATCHING FOR ME. Concluded.

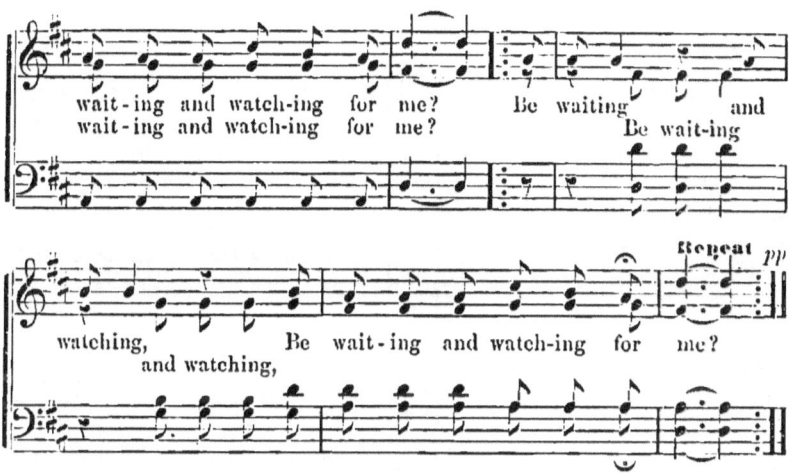

No. 88. LOVING SAVIOR, ONLY THEE.

"Whom have I in heaven but thee?"—Ps. lxxiii: 25.

FANNY J. CROSBY.   W. H. DOANE, by per.

1. On - ly Thee, my soul's Redeemer! Whom have I in heaven beside?
2. On - ly Thee! no joy I co - vet But the joy to call Thee mine—
3. On - ly Thee! I ask no oth - er, Thou art more than all to me;
4. Only Thee, whose blood has cleansed me, Would my raptured vision see,

Who on earth, with love so ten - der, All my wand'ring steps will guide.
Joy that gives the blest assurance, Thou hast owned and sealed me Thine
Life, or health, or creature comfort,—I would give them all for Thee.
While my faith is reaching up-ward, Ev - er upward, Lord, to Thee.

REFRAIN.

On - ly Thee, on - ly Thee, Lov - ing Sav - ior, on - ly Thee.

No. 91. WEEPING WILL NOT SAVE ME.

"For by grace are ye saved through faith."—Eph. ii: 8.

R. L. R. LOWRY, by per.

1. Weeping will not save me—Tho' my face were bathed in tears, That could not allay my fears, Could not wash the sins of years—Weeping will not save me.
2. Working will not save me—Purest deeds that I can do, Holiest thought and feelings too, Can not form my soul a-new—Working will not save me.
3. Waiting will not save me—Helpless, guilty, lost I lie; In my ear is mercy's cry; If I wait I can but die—Waiting will not save me.
4. Faith in Christ will save me—Let me trust Thy weeping Son; Trust the work that He has done; To His arms, Lord, help me run—Faith in Christ will save me.

REFRAIN.

Je-sus wept and died for me; Je-sus suf-fered on the tree; Je-sus waits to make me free, He a-lone can save me.

No. 92. OUR BETTER HOME BEYOND.

"Now they desire a better country."—Heb. xi: 16.

FANNY J. CROSBY. W. H. DOANE, by per.

Andante. May be sung as a Duet.

1. Had earth no thorns among its flow'rs, And life no fount of tears,
2. How wise-ly God our cup has filled With mingled joy and grief,
3. Our bet-ter home! how sweet to think, When torn from those we love,
4. Oh, bliss-ful moment, when a-side These earthly robes we'll cast,

We might for-get our bet-ter home Be-yond this vale of tears.
To teach our hearts that mortal things, Tho' bright, are on-ly brief.
No sad fare-well can ev-er reach Our bet-ter home a-bove.
Then wake to know our souls have found The bet-ter home at last.

REFRAIN.

Home, sweet home, . . . Our beau-ti-ful home be-yond; Our
Beau-ti-ful home,

home that Je-sus has gone to prepare, Our beautiful home be-yond.

WE'LL MEET AGAIN. Concluded.

REFRAIN.

Yes, we'll meet a-gain, Yes, we'll meet a-gain; In heaven a-bove, where all is love, We'll meet, we'll meet a-gain.

No. 94. CONSECRATE ME, LORD.

"Consecrate yourselves this day to the Lord."—Ex. xxxii: 29.

F. R. HAVERGAL. W. H. D.

1. Take my life, and let it be Con-se-cra-ted, Lord, to Thee;
2. Take my hands, and let them be Swift and beau-ti-ful for Thee;
3. Take my lips, and let them be Filled with mes-sa-ges from Thee;
4. Take my in-tel-lect and use Every power as Thou shalt choose;
5. Take my love, my Lord, I pour At Thy feet its *treas-ure-store*;

Take my mo-ments and my days, Let them flow in ceaseless praise.
Take my voice, and let me sing Al-ways on-ly for my King.
Take my sil-ver and my gold, Not a mite would I be-hold.
Take my will, and make it Thine, It shall be no lon-ger mine.
Take my-self, and I will be Ev-er, on-ly, *all for Thee.*

No. 95. TELL ME THE OLD, OLD STORY.

"Tell them how great things the Lord hath done."—Mark v: 19.

Miss KATE HANKEY.   W. H. DOANE, by per.

1. Tell me the Old, Old sto-ry Of unseen things a-bove, Of Je-sus and His glo-ry, Of Je-sus and His love. Tell me the Story sim-ply, As to a lit-tle child, For I am weak and wea-ry, And help-less and de-filed.

2. Tell me the Sto-ry slow-ly, That I may take it in— That wonder-ful re-demp-tion, God's rem-e-dy for sin. Tell me the Story oft-en, For I for-get so soon, The "early dew" of morn-ing Has passed a-way at noon.

3. Tell me the same Old Sto-ry, When you have cause to fear That this world's empty glo-ry Is cost-ing me too dear. Yes, and when that world's glo-ry Is dawning on my soul, Tell me the Old, Old Sto-ry, "Christ Jesus makes thee whole."

REFRAIN.

Tell me the Old, Old Sto-ry, Tell me the Old, Old Sto-ry, Tell me the Old, Old Sto-ry Of Je-sus and His love.

No. 96. REACH ME THY HAND.

"With a true heart in full assurance of faith."—Heb. x: 22.

Mrs. E. H. GATES. W. H. DOANE, by per.

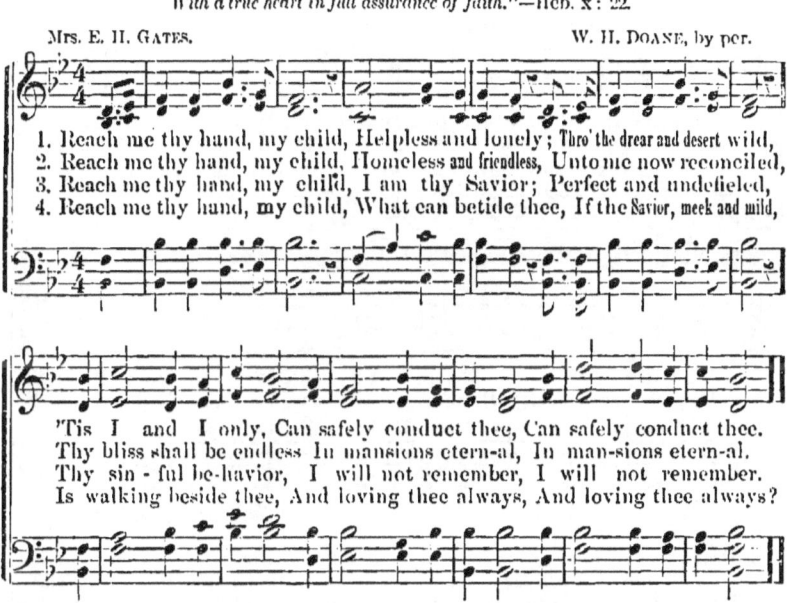

1. Reach me thy hand, my child, Helpless and lonely; Thro' the drear and desert wild,
2. Reach me thy hand, my child, Homeless and friendless, Unto me now reconciled,
3. Reach me thy hand, my child, I am thy Savior; Perfect and undefiled,
4. Reach me thy hand, my child, What can betide thee, If the Savior, meek and mild,

'Tis I and I only, Can safely conduct thee, Can safely conduct thee.
Thy bliss shall be endless In mansions etern-al, In man-sions etern-al.
Thy sin-ful be-havior, I will not remember, I will not remember.
Is walking beside thee, And loving thee always, And loving thee always?

No. 97. O LAMB OF GOD, STILL KEEP ME.

"And thou shalt take thy rest in safety."—Job xi: 18.

J. G. DECK, 1857. From "Songs of Devotion," by per.

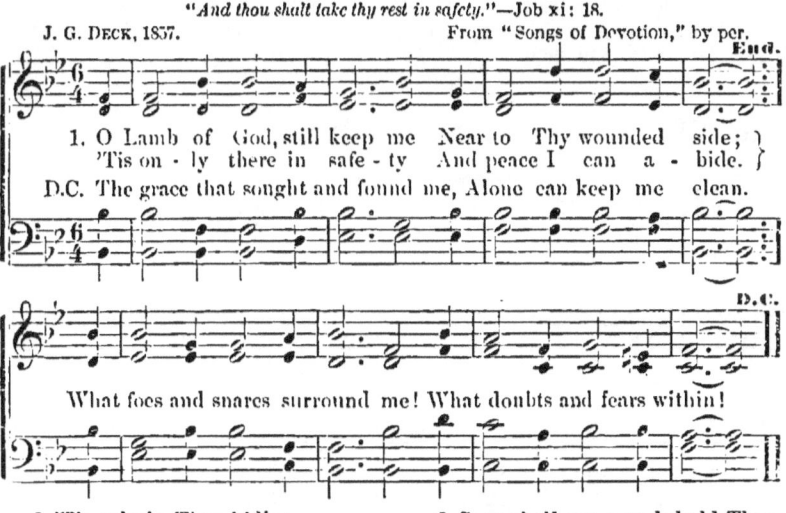

1. O Lamb of God, still keep me Near to Thy wounded side;
   'Tis on-ly there in safe-ty And peace I can a-bide.
D.C. The grace that sought and found me, Alone can keep me clean.

What foes and snares surround me! What doubts and fears within!

2 'Tis only in Thee hiding,
   I feel my life secure;
  Only in Thee abiding,
   The conflict can endure.
  Thine arm the victory gaineth
   O'er every hateful foe;
  Thy love my heart sustaineth
   In all its care and woe.

3 Soon shall my eyes behold Thee,
   With rapture, face to face;
  One-half hath not been told me
   Of all Thy power and grace.
  Thy beauty, Lord, and glory,
   The wonders of Thy love,
  Shall be the endless story
   Of all Thy saints above.

No. 98.   IN THAT HAPPY LAND.

Arr. by W. H. D.

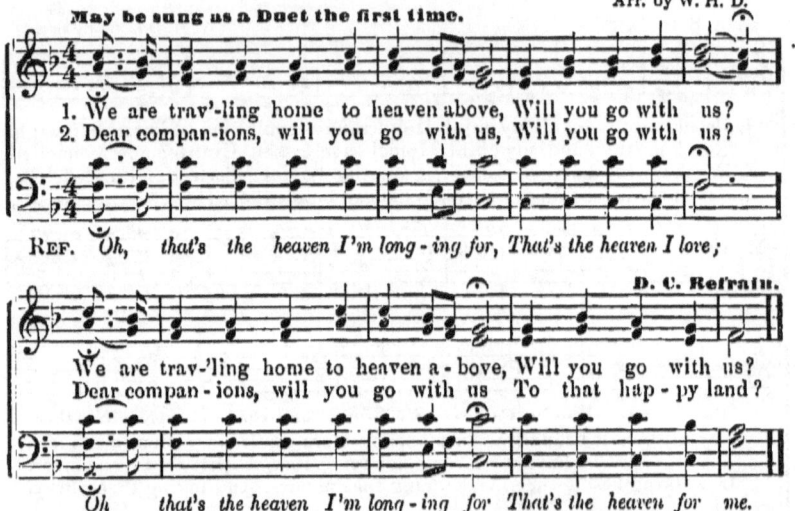

1. We are trav'-ling home to heaven above, Will you go with us?
2. Dear compan-ions, will you go with us, Will you go with us?

REF. Oh, that's the heaven I'm long-ing for, That's the heaven I love;

D. C. Refrain.

We are trav-'ling home to heaven a-bove, Will you go with us?
Dear compan-ions, will you go with us To that hap-py land?

Oh, that's the heaven I'm long-ing for That's the heaven for me.

3 Dear parents, will you go with us,
  Will you go with us?
  Dear parents, will you go with us,
  To that happy land?

4 Let us meet, dear children, in that
  In that happy land;   [land,
  Let us meet, dear children, in that
  In that happy land.   [land,

5 Let us meet, dear parents, in that
  In that happy land;   [land,
  Let us meet, dear parents, in that
  In that happy land.   [land.

6 Our Savior He will lead us on!
  Will you go with us?
  Our Savior He will lead us on!
  Will you go with us?

No. 99.   COME TO JESUS.

1. Come to Je-sus, come to Je-sus, Come to Je-sus, just now, just now, Come to Je-sus, come to Je-sus, just now.

2 He will save you.
3 Oh, believe Him.
4 He is able.
5 He is willing.
6 He'll receive you.

7 Call upon Him.
8 He will hear you.
9 Look unto Him.
10 He'll forgive you.
11 Flee to Jesus.

12 He will cleanse you.
13 He will clothe you.
14 Jesus loves you.
15 Don't reject Him.
16 Only trust Him.

No. 100. THERE IS A FOUNTAIN.

Cowper, 1779. Old Melody.

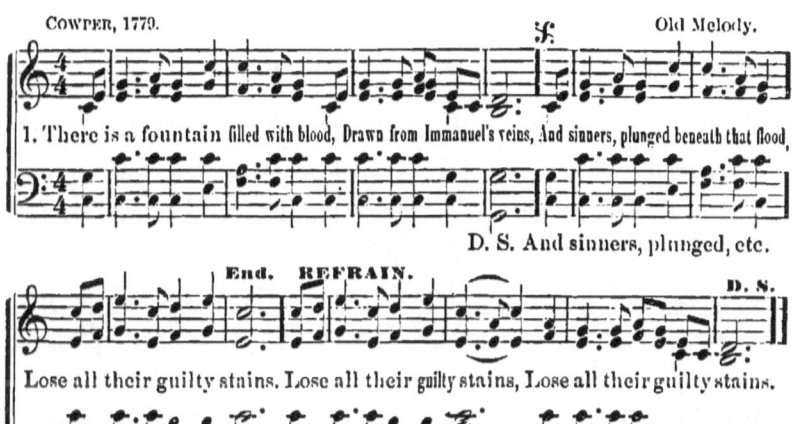

1. There is a fountain filled with blood, Drawn from Immanuel's veins, And sinners, plunged beneath that flood,

D. S. And sinners, plunged, etc.

Lose all their guilty stains. Lose all their guilty stains, Lose all their guilty stains.

2 The dying thief rejoiced to see
 That fountain in his day;
And there may I, though vile as he,
 Wash all my sins away.

3 Dear dying Lamb! thy precious blood
 Shall never lose its power,
Till all the ransomed Church of God
 Are saved to sin no more.

4 E'er since, by faith, I saw the stream
 Thy flowing wounds supply,
Redeeming love has been my theme,
 And shall be, till I die.

5 And when this feeble, stam'ring tongue
 Lies silent in the grave,
Then, in a nobler, sweeter song,
 I'll sing thy power to save.

No. 101. WE PRAISE THEE, O GOD.

1. We praise Thee, O God! for the Son of Thy love, For Jesus who died, and is now gone above.
2. We praise Thee, O God! for Thy Spirit of light, Who has shown us our Savior, and scattered our night.

REFRAIN.

{ Hallelujah! Thine the glory, Halle-lujah! A-men.
{ Hallelujah! Thine the glory, ... } Revive us a-gain.

3 All glory and praise to the Lamb
 that was slain,
Who has borne all our sins, and has
 cleansed every stain.

4 Revive us again; fill each heart with
 Thy love;
May each soul be rekindled with fire
 from above.

No. 102. COME THOU FOUNT. (Nettleton.)

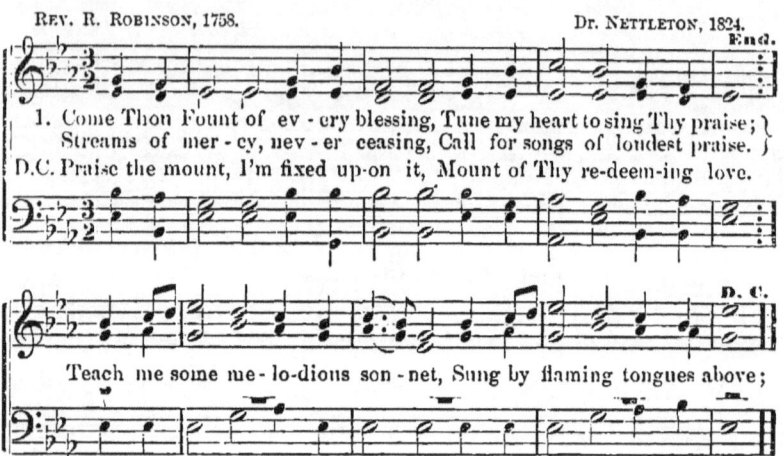

2 Here I raise my Ebenezer,
  Hither by Thy help I'm come,
And I hope, by Thy good pleasure,
  Safely to arrive at home.
Jesus sought me when a stranger,
  Wandering from the fold of God,
He, to rescue me from danger,
  Interposed His precious blood.

2 Oh, to grace how great a debtor,
  Daily I'm constrained to be!
Let thy goodness, like a fetter,
  Bind my wandering heart to Thee.
Prone to wander, Lord, I feel it,
  Prone to leave the God I love,
Here's my heart, oh, take and seal it,
  Seal it for Thy courts above.

No. 103. ALL HAIL THE POWER. (Coronation.)

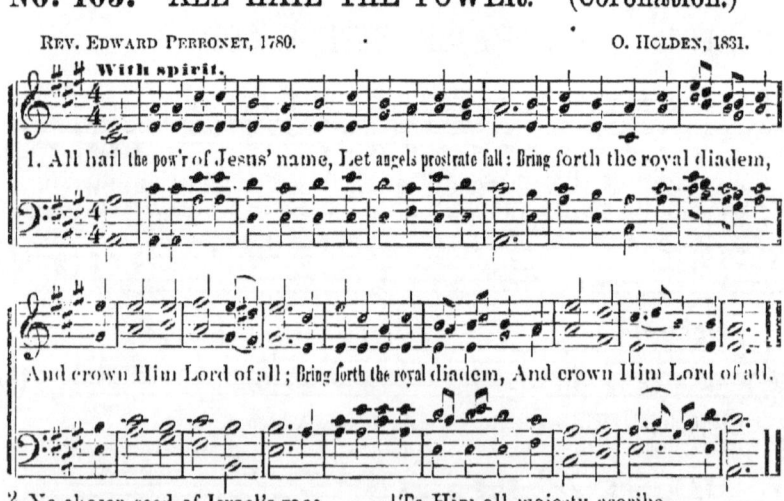

2 Ye chosen seed of Israel's race,
  Ye ransomed from the fall,
Hail Him who saves you by His grace,
  And crown Him Lord of all.

3 Let every kindred, every tribe,
  On this terrestrial ball,

To Him all majesty ascribe,
  And crown Him Lord of all.

4 Oh, that with yonder sacred throng
  We at His feet may fall;
We'll join the everlasting song,
  And crown Him Lord of all.

No. 104. **THERE IS A NAME I LOVE.**

"*I will bless thy name forever.*"—Ps. cxlv ; 2.

From "Songs of Devotion," by per.

1. There is a name I love to hear, I love to speak its worth;
It sounds like mu-sic in mine ear, The sweetest name on earth.
2. It tells me of a Sav-ior's love, Who died to set me free;
It tells me of His precious blood, The sinner's per-fect plea.

D. C. *No saint on earth its worth can tell, No heart con - ceive how dear!*

REFRAIN.

Je-sus! the name I love so well, The name I love to hear!

3 It tells of one whose loving heart
Can feel my deepest woe,
Who in my sorrow bears a part
That none can bear below.

4 It bids my trembling heart rejoice,
It dries each rising tear;
It tells me, in a "still small voice,"
To trust and never fear.

No. 105. **JUST AS I AM.**

CHARLOTTE ELLIOTT, 1836.   GREGORIAN.

1. Just as I am, without one plea, But that Thy blood was shed for me,
2. Just as I am, though tossed about With many a conflict, many a doubt,
3. Just as I am—Thy love unknown, Has broken ev-ery barrier down;

REF. Just as I am, I come, I come, Yea, to be Thine, I come, I come;

D. C. Refrain.

And that Thou bid'st me come to Thee, O Lamb of God, I come, I come!
Fighting within, and fears with-out, O Lamb of God, I come, I come!
Now to be Thine, yea, Thine a-lone, O Lamb of God, I come, I come!

Now to be Thine, yea, Thine a - lone, O Lamb of God, I come, I come!

No. 106. BROAD IS THE ROAD.

Windham. L. M.   Daniel Read. 1785.

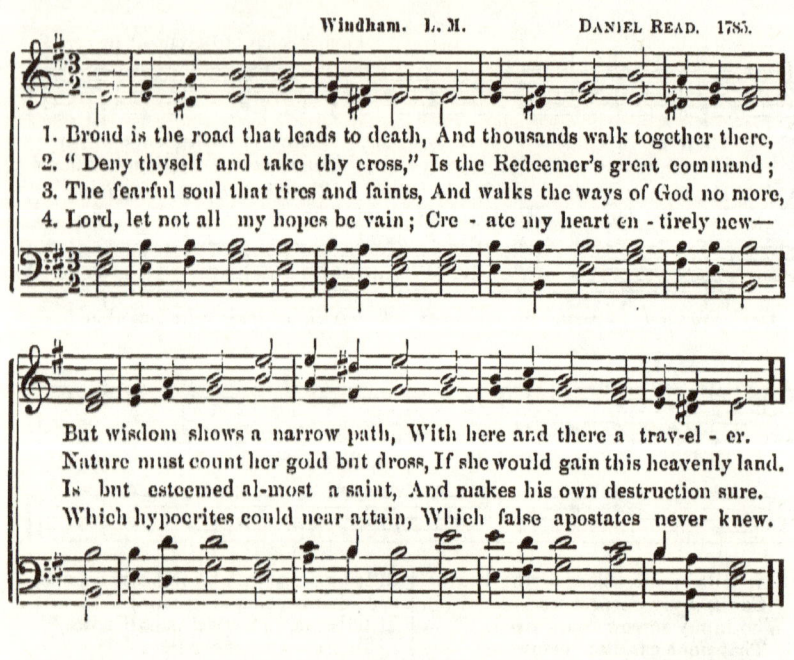

1. Broad is the road that leads to death, And thousands walk together there,
2. "Deny thyself and take thy cross," Is the Redeemer's great command;
3. The fearful soul that tires and faints, And walks the ways of God no more,
4. Lord, let not all my hopes be vain; Cre - ate my heart en - tirely new—

But wisdom shows a narrow path, With here and there a trav-el - er.
Nature must count her gold but dross, If she would gain this heavenly land.
Is but esteemed al-most a saint, And makes his own destruction sure.
Which hypocrites could near attain, Which false apostates never knew.

No. 107. BEHOLD A STRANGER AT THE DOOR.

Rev. Joseph Grigg, 1765.   Woodworth. L. M.   Wm. B. Bradbury, 1849.

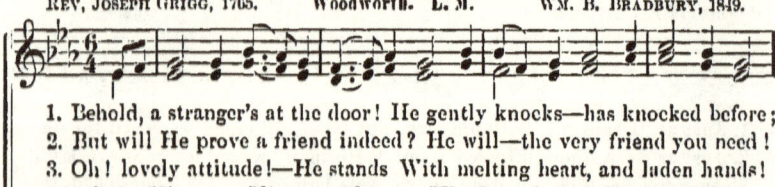

1. Behold, a stranger's at the door! He gently knocks—has knocked before;
2. But will He prove a friend indeed? He will—the very friend you need!
3. Oh! lovely attitude!—He stands With melting heart, and laden hands!
4. Admit Him, ere His anger burn— His feet departed ne'er return;

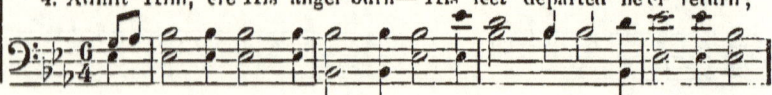

Has waited long—is waiting still; You treat no other friend so ill.
The Man of Nazareth!—'tis He, With garments dyed at Calva - ry.
Oh! matchless kindness!—and He shows This matchless kindness to His foes.
Admit Him, or the hour's at hand When at His door denied you'll stand.

No. 108. FROM EVERY STORMY WIND.

Rev. Hugh Stowell, 1832.   Retreat. L. M.   T. Hastings, 1840.

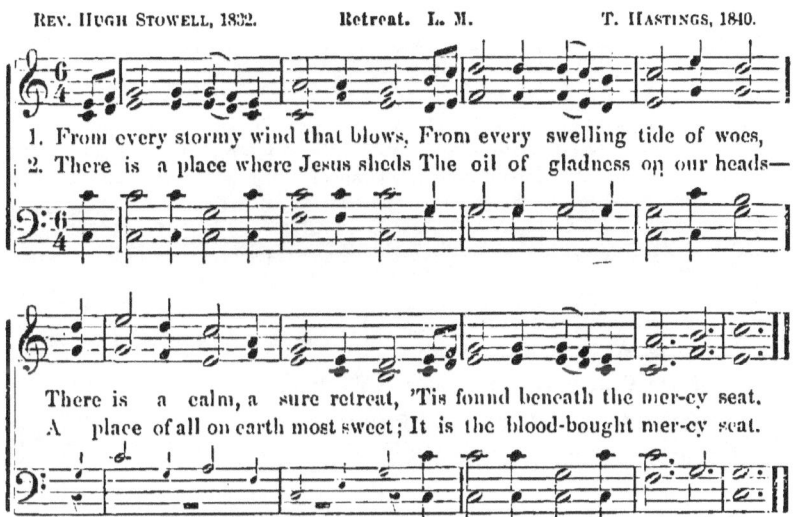

1. From every stormy wind that blows, From every swelling tide of woes, There is a calm, a sure retreat, 'Tis found beneath the mer-cy seat.
2. There is a place where Jesus sheds The oil of gladness on our heads— A place of all on earth most sweet; It is the blood-bought mer-cy seat.

3 There is a scene where spirits blend,
Where friend holds fellowship with friend;
Tho' sundered far, by faith they meet
Around one common mercy seat.

4 There, there on eagle wings we soar,
And sin and sense molest no more;
And heaven comes down our souls to greet,
And glory crowns the mercy seat.

No. 109. OH, FOR A CLOSER WALK.

William Cowper, 1779.   Ortonville. C. M.   Dr. Hastings, 1837.

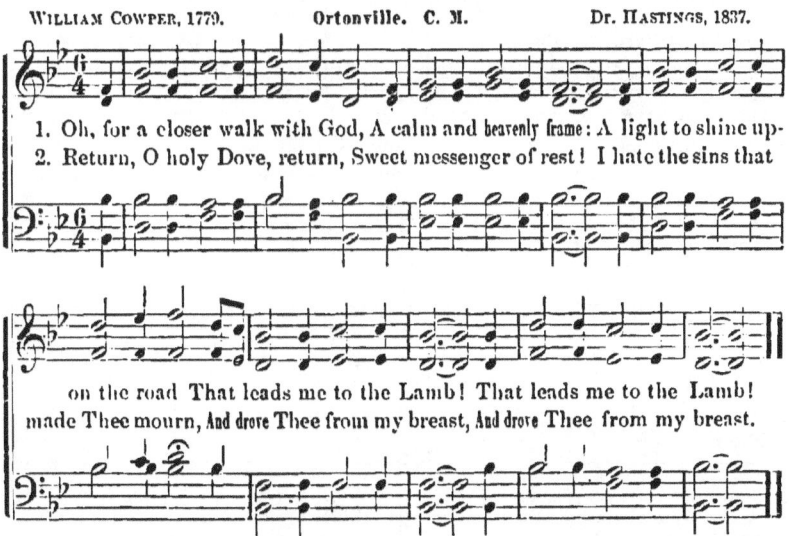

1. Oh, for a closer walk with God, A calm and heavenly frame: A light to shine upon the road That leads me to the Lamb! That leads me to the Lamb!
2. Return, O holy Dove, return, Sweet messenger of rest! I hate the sins that made Thee mourn, And drove Thee from my breast, And drove Thee from my breast.

3 The dearest idol I have known,
    Whate'er that idol be,
Help me to tear it from Thy throne,
    And worship only Thee.

4 So shall my walk be close with God,
    Calm and serene my frame;
So purer light shall mark the road
    That leads me to the Lamb.

No. 110. JESUS, LOVER OF MY SOUL.

Rev. Charles Wesley, 1740.   MARTYN. 7.   S. B. Marsh, 1834.

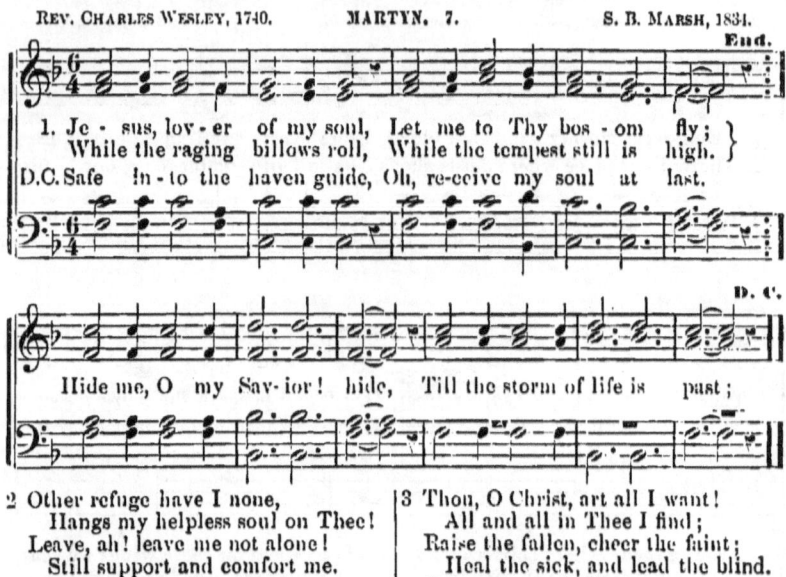

1. Jesus, lover of my soul, Let me to Thy bosom fly;
While the raging billows roll, While the tempest still is high.
D.C. Safe into the haven guide, Oh, receive my soul at last.
Hide me, O my Savior! hide, Till the storm of life is past;

2 Other refuge have I none,
  Hangs my helpless soul on Thee!
  Leave, ah! leave me not alone!
  Still support and comfort me.
  All my trust on Thee is stayed;
  All my help from Thee I bring;
  Cover my defenseless head
  With the shadow of Thy wing.

3 Thou, O Christ, art all I want!
  All and all in Thee I find;
  Raise the fallen, cheer the faint;
  Heal the sick, and lead the blind.
  Just and holy is Thy name;
  I am all unrighteousness;
  Vile, and full of sin I am;
  Thou art full of truth and grace.

No. 111. ROCK OF AGES.

Rev. A. M. Toplady, 1776.   Dr. Hastings, 1830.

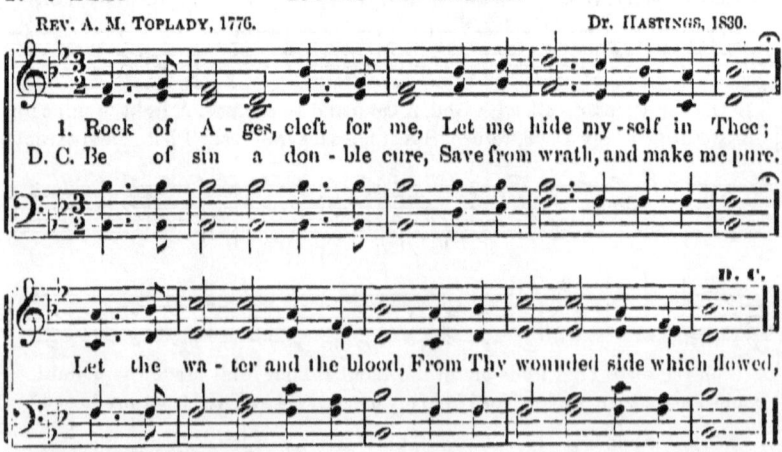

1. Rock of Ages, cleft for me, Let me hide myself in Thee;
D. C. Be of sin a double cure, Save from wrath, and make me pure.
Let the water and the blood, From Thy wounded side which flowed,

2 Could my tears forever flow,
  Could my zeal no languor know,
  This for sin could not atone,
  Thou must save, and Thou alone;
  In my hand no price I bring,
  Simply to Thy cross I cling.

3 While I draw this fleeting breath,
  When my eyes shall close in death,
  When I rise to worlds unknown,
  And behold Thee on Thy throne,
  Rock of Ages, cleft for me,
  Let me hide myself in Thee.

No. 112. BLEST BE THE TIE.

Rev. J. Fawcett, 1772. Dennis. S. M. H. G. Nageli, 1832.

1. Blest be the tie that binds Our hearts in Chris-tian love;
2. Be-fore our Fa-ther's throne, We pour our ar-dent prayers:
3. We share our mu-tual woes; Our mu-tual bur-dens bear;

The fel-low-ship of kin-dred minds Is like to that a-bove.
Our fears, our hopes, our aims are one, Our comforts and our cares.
And oft-en for each oth-er flows The sym-pathiz-ing tear.

4 When we asunder part,
  It gives us inward pain ;
  But we shall still be joined in heart,
  And hope to meet again.

5 This glorious hope revives
  Our courage by the way ;
  While each in expectation lives,
  And longs to see the day.

No. 113. COME, SAID JESUS.

Mrs. A. L. Barbauld, 1825. Horton. 7. X. S. Von Wartensee, 1786.

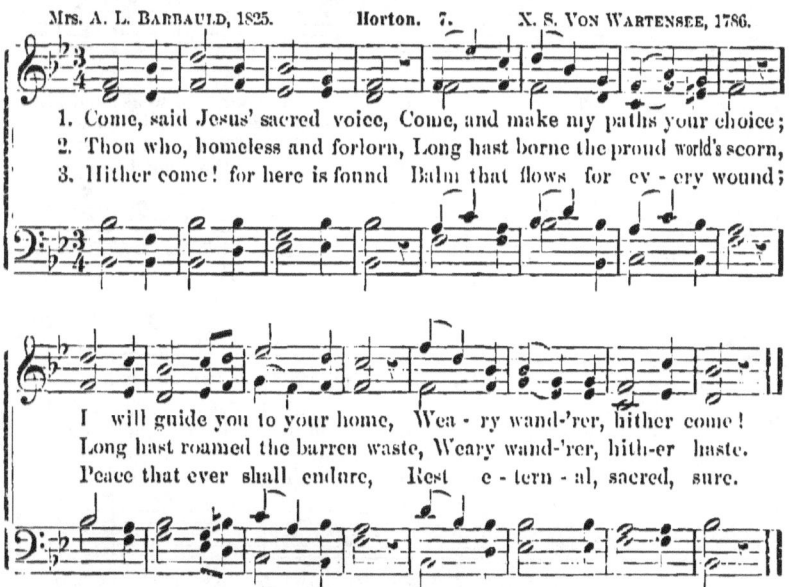

1. Come, said Jesus' sacred voice, Come, and make my paths your choice;
2. Thou who, homeless and forlorn, Long hast borne the proud world's scorn,
3. Hither come! for here is found Balm that flows for ev-ery wound;

I will guide you to your home, Wea-ry wand'rer, hither come!
Long hast roamed the barren waste, Weary wand'rer, hith-er haste.
Peace that ever shall endure, Rest e-ter-nal, sacred, sure.

No. 114. OH, TURN YE, OH, TURN YE.

Epostulation. 11.   Rev. Josiah Hopkins, 1830.

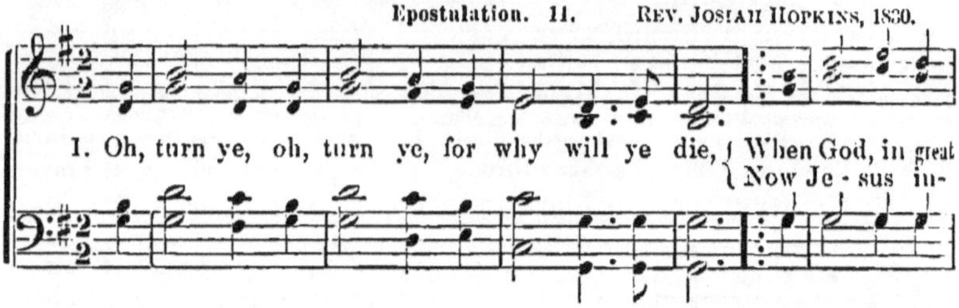

1. Oh, turn ye, oh, turn ye, for why will ye die, { When God, in great mercy is coming so nigh? }
{ Now Je-sus invites you, the Spirit says, Come! } And angels are waiting to welcome you home.

2 And now Christ is ready your souls to receive,
Oh! how can you question, if you will believe?
If sin is your burden, why will you not come?
'Tis you He bids welcome; He bids you come home.

3 Though clouds may surround us, our God is our light;
Though storms rage around us, our God is our might;
So faint, yet pursuing, still onward we come;
The Lord is our leader, and heaven is our home!

No. 115. I AM TRUSTING, LORD, IN THEE.

W. McDonald.   Wm. G. Fischer, by per.

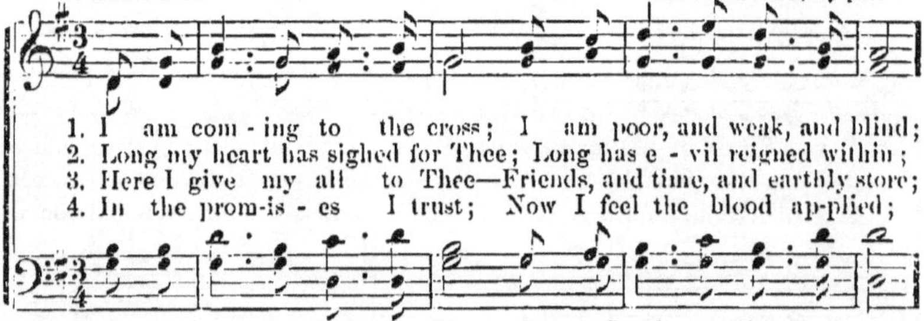

1. I am com-ing to the cross; I am poor, and weak, and blind;
2. Long my heart has sighed for Thee; Long has e-vil reigned within;
3. Here I give my all to Thee—Friends, and time, and earthly store;
4. In the prom-is-es I trust; Now I feel the blood ap-plied;

Ref. I am trust-ing, Lord, in Thee, Dear Lamb of Cal-va-ry;

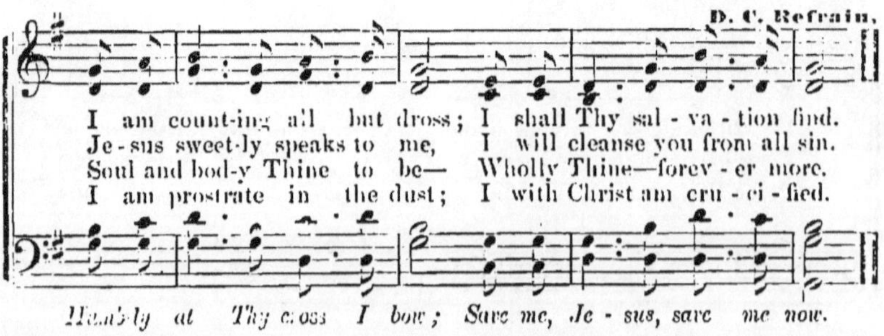

D. C. Refrain.

I am count-ing all but dross; I shall Thy sal-va-tion find.
Je-sus sweet-ly speaks to me, I will cleanse you from all sin.
Soul and bod-y Thine to be— Wholly Thine—forev-er more.
I am prostrate in the dust; I with Christ am cru-ci-fied.

Humbly at Thy cross I bow; Save me, Je-sus, save me now.

116 What a friend in Jesus.

1 What a Friend we have in Jesus,
　All our sins and griefs to bear;
　What a privilege to carry
　Every thing to God in prayer.
　Oh, what peace we often forfeit,
　Oh, what needless pain we bear—
　All because we do not carry
　Every thing to God in prayer.

2 Have we trials and temptations?
　Is there trouble anywhere?
　We should never be discouraged,
　Take it to the Lord in prayer.
　Can we find a Friend so faithful,
　Who will all our sorrows share?
　Jesus knows our every weakness,
　Take it to the Lord in prayer.

3 Are we weak and heavy laden,
　Cumbered with a load of care?
　Precious Savior, still our refuge—
　Take it to the Lord in prayer.
　Do thy friends despise, forsake thee?
　Take it to the Lord in prayer.
　In His arms He'll take and shield thee,
　Thou wilt find a solace there.

117 Cross and Crown. C. M.

1 Must Jesus bear the cross alone,
　And all the world go free?
　No, there's a cross for every one,
　And there's a cross for me.

2 How happy are the saints above
　Who once went sorrowing here;
　But now they taste unmingled love,
　And joy without a tear.

3 The consecrated cross I'll bear
　Till death shall set me free,
　And then go home my crown to wear—
　For there's a crown for me!

118 Pleyel's Hymn. 7.

1 Haste, O sinner, now be wise;
　Stay not for the morrow's sun;
　Wisdom if you still despise,
　Harder is it to be won.

2 Haste, and mercy now implore;
　Stay not for the morrow's sun,
　Lest thy season should be o'er,
　Ere this evening's stage be run.

3 Haste, O sinner, now return;
　Stay not for the morrow's sun,
　Lest thy lamp should cease to burn
　Ere salvation's work is done.

119 Invitation. 8. 7. 4.

1 Come, ye sinners, poor and needy,
　Weak and wounded, sick and sore;
　Jesus ready stands to save you,
　Full of pity, love and power,
　　He is able,
　He is willing, doubt no more.

2 Come, ye thirsty, come and welcome;
　God's free bounty glorify;
　True belief and true repentance,
　Every grace that brings us nigh—
　　Without money,
　Come to Jesus Christ and buy.

3 Come, ye weary, heavy laden,
　Lost and ruined by the fall,
　If you tarry till you're better,
　You will never come at all.
　　Not the righteous—
　Sinners, Jesus came to call.

4 Let not conscience make you linger,
　Nor of fitness fondly dream;
　All the fitness he requireth
　Is to feel your need of him;
　　This he gives you—
　'Tis the Spirit's rising beam.

120 Waiting by the River.

1 Tho' the mist hang o'er the river,
　And its billows loudly roar,
　Yet we hear the song of angels
　Wafted from the other shore.

Cho.—We are waiting by the river,
　We are watching on the shore,
　Only waiting for the angels,
　Soon they'll come to bear us o'er.

2 He has called for many a loved one,
　We have seen them leave our side;
　With our Savior we shall meet them
　When we, too, have crossed the tide.

3 When we've passed that vale of shadows,
　With its dark and chilling tide,
　In that bright and glorious city
　We shall evermore abide.

121 State Street. S. M.

1 The Spirit in our hearts
　Is whispering, "Sinner, come;".
The bride, the church of Christ, proclaims
　To all His children, "Come!"

2 Let him that heareth say
　To all about him, "Come!"
　Let him that thirsts for righteousness
　To Christ, the fountain, come.

122 Boylston. S. M.

1 Did Christ o'er sinners weep?
    And shall our cheeks be dry?
  Let floods of penitential grief
    Burst forth from every eye.

2 The Son of God in tears
    The wond'ring angels see;
  Be thou astonished, O my soul;
    He shed those tears for thee.

3 He wept that we might weep;
    Each sin demands a tear;
  In heaven alone no sin is found,
    And there's no weeping there.

123 Peterboro. C. M.

1 Oh, for a faith that will not shrink,
    Though pressed by every foe,
  That will not tremble on the brink
    Of any earthly woe!

2 A faith that shines more bright and clear
    When tempests rage without;
  That when in danger knows no fear,
    In darkness feels no doubt.

3 Lord, give us such a faith as this,
    And then, whate'er may come,
  We'll taste, e'en here, the hallowed bliss
    Of an eternal home.

124 Bethany. 6. 4.

1 Nearer, my God, to thee,
    Nearer to thee!
  E'en though it be a cross
    That raiseth me.
  Still all my song shall be
  Nearer, my God, to thee,
    Nearer to thee!

2 Though like a wanderer,
    Daylight all gone,
  Darkness be over me,
    My rest a stone;
  Yet in my dreams I'd be
  Nearer, my God, to thee,
    Nearer to thee!

3 There let my way appear
    Steps unto heaven;
  All that thou sendest me
    In mercy given;
  Angels to beckon me
  Nearer, my God, to thee,
    Nearer to thee!

125 Naomi. C. M.

1 Father, whate'er of earthly bliss
    Thy sovereign will denies,
  Accepted at thy throne of grace,
    Let this petition rise:

2 Give me a calm, a thankful heart,
    From every murmur free;
  The blessings of thy grace impart,
    And make me live to thee.

3 Let the sweet hope that thou art mine
    My life and death attend;
  Thy presence through my journey shine,
    And crown my journey's end.

126 The solid rock. L. M.

1 My hope is built on nothing less
  Than Jesus' blood and righteousness:
  I dare not trust the sweetest frame,
  But wholly lean on Jesus' name;
    On Christ, the solid rock, I stand;
    All other ground is sinking sand.

2 When darkness seems to vail his face,
  I rest on his unchanging grace;
  In every high and stormy gale
  My anchor holds within the vail;
    On Christ, the solid rock, I stand;
    All other ground is sinking sand.

127 I do believe. C. M.

1 Father, I stretch my hands to thee,
    No other help I know;
  If thou withdraw thyself from me,
    Ah, whither shall I go?

CHORUS:

  I do believe, I now believe,
    That Jesus died for me;
  And through his blood, his precious blood,
    I shall from sin be free.

2 What did thine only Son endure
    Before I drew my breath!
  What pain, what labor, to secure
    My soul from endless death.

3 Author of faith, to thee I lift
    My weary, longing eyes,
  Oh may I now receive that gift—
    My soul, without it, dies.

128 Sweet hour of prayer.

1 Sweet hour of prayer, sweet hour of
prayer,
That calls me from a world of care,
And bids me at my Father's throne
Make all my wants and wishes known;
In seasons of distress and grief,
My soul has often found relief,
And oft escaped the tempter's snare
By thy return, sweet hour of prayer.

2 Sweet hour of prayer, sweet hour of
prayer,
Thy wing shall my petition bear
To him, whose truth and faithfulness
Engage the waiting soul to bless.
And since he bids me seek his face,
Believe his word and trust his grace,
I'll cast on him my every care,
And wait for thee, sweet hour of prayer.

129 My Jesus, I love thee.

1 My Jesus, I love thee, I know thou art
mine,
For thee all the pleasures of sin I resign;
My gracious Redeemer, my Savior art
thou,
‖:If ever I loved thee,:‖ my Jesus 'tis now.

2 I love thee, because thou hast first loved
me,
And purchased my pardon on Calvary's
tree;
I love thee for wearing the thorns on thy
brow,
‖:If ever I loved thee,:‖ my Jesus, 'tis now.

130 He leadeth me.

1 He leadeth me! O blessed thought,
Oh, words with heavenly comfort fraught
Whate'er I do, where'er I be,
Still 'tis God's hand that leadeth me!

REFRAIN.

He leadeth me! he leadeth me!
By his own hand he leadeth me;
His faithful follower I would be,
For by his hand he leadeth me.

2 Lord, I would clasp thy hand in mine,
Nor ever murmur nor repine,
Content, whatever lot I see,
Since 'tis my God that leadeth me.

131 Shepard. 8. 7. 4.

1 Savior, like a shepherd lead us,
  Much we need thy tenderest care;
In thy pleasant pastures feed us,
  For our use thy folds prepare.
    Blessed Jesus,
Thou hast bound us, thine we are.

2 Thou hast promised to receive us,
  Poor and sinful though we be;
Thou hast mercy to relieve us,
  Grace to cleanse, and power to free;
    Blessed Jesus,
Let us early turn to thee.

3 Early let us seek thy favor,
  Early let us do thy will;
Blessed Lord and only Savior,
  With thy love our bosom fill;
    Blessed Jesus,
Thou hast loved us, love us still.

132 Arlington. C. M.

1 Come, Holy Spirit, heavenly dove,
  With all thy quick'ning powers;
Kindle a flame of sacred love
  In these cold hearts of ours.

2 In vain we tune our formal songs,
  In vain we strive to rise;
Hosannas languish on our tongues,
  And our devotion dies.

3 Father, and shall we ever live
  At this poor dying rate;
Our love so faint, so cold to thee,
  And thine to us so great?

4 Come, Holy Spirit, heavenly Dove,
  With all thy quick'ning powers;
Come, shed abroad a Savior's love,
  And that shall kindle ours.

133 Even me. 8. 7. 3.

1 Lord, I hear of show'rs of blessing
  Thou art scatt'ring full and free—
Show'rs, the thirsty land refreshing,
  Let some droppings fall on me—
    Even me.

2 Pass me not, O God, our Father!
  Sinful though my heart may be,
Thou might'st leave me, but the rather
  Let thy mercy light on me—
    Even me.

3 Pass me not, O gracious Savior!
  Let me live and cling to thee,
For I'm longing for thy favor;
  Whilst thou art calling, oh call me—
    Even me.

134. The sweetest name. C. M.

1 There is no name so sweet on earth,
  No name so sweet in heaven—
  The name before his wondrous birth
    To Christ the Savior given.
  We love to sing around our King,
    And hail him blessed Jesus;
  For there's no word ear ever heard
    So dear, so sweet, as Jesus.

2 And when he hung upon the tree,
  They wrote this name above him,
  That all might see the reason we
    For evermore must love him.
    We love to sing, etc.

3 So now, upon his Father's throne,
  Almighty to release us
  From sin and pains, he ever reigns,
    The Prince and Savior, Jesus.
    We love to sing, etc.

135. Windham. L. M.

1 Show pity, Lord, O Lord forgive,
  Let a repenting rebel live;
  Are not thy mercies large and free?
  May not a sinner trust in thee?

2 My crimes are great, but do n't surpass
  The power and glory of thy grace;
  Great God, thy nature hath no bound,
  So let thy pard'ning love be found.

3 O wash my soul from every sin,
  And make my guilty conscience clean;
  Here on my heart the burden lies,
  And past offenses pain my eyes.

4 Yet save a trembling sinner, Lord,
  Whose hope, still hovering round thy word,
  Would light on some sweet promise there,
  Some sure support against despair.

136. Naomi. C. M.

1 Oh, could I find, from day to day,
    A nearness to my God;
  Then would my hours glide sweet away
    While leaning on his word.

2 Lord, I desire with thee to live
    Anew from day to day,
  In joys the world can never give,
    Nor ever take away.

3 Blest Jesus, come and rule my heart,
    And make me wholly thine,
  That I may never more depart,
    Nor grieve thy love divine.

137. Water of life.

1 Jesus the water of life will give,
    Freely, freely, freely,
  Jesus the water of life will give,
    Freely to those who love him.
  Come to that fountain, O drink and live,
    Freely, freely, freely,
  Come to that fountain, O drink and live,
    Flowing for those that love him.

CHORUS:

The Spirit and the Bride say come,
  Freely, freely, freely,
And he that is thirsty let him come,
  And drink of the water of life.
The fountain of life is flowing,
  Flowing, freely, flowing;
The fountain of life is flowing,
  Is flowing for you and for me.

2 Jesus has promised a home in heaven,
    Freely, freely, freely,
  Jesus has promised a home in heaven,
    Freely to those that love him.
  Treasures unfading will there be given,
    Freely, freely, freely,
  Treasures unfading will there be given,
    Freely to those that love him.

138. Jesus of Nazareth.

1 What means this eager, anxious throng,
  Pressing our busy streets along—
  These wondrous gatherings day by day?
  What means this strange commotion, pray?
  ||:Voices in accents hushed, reply,
  "Jesus of Nazareth passeth by!":||

2 E'en children feel the potent spell,
  And haste their new-found joy to tell;
  In crowds they to the place repair,
  Where Christians daily bow in prayer.
  ||:Hosannas mingle with the cry,
  "Jesus of Nazareth passeth by!":||

3 Ho, all ye heavy laden, come!
  Here's pardon, comfort, rest, a home;
  Lost wanderers from a Father's face,
  Return, accept His proffered grace!
  ||:Ye tempted! there's a refuge nigh,
  "Jesus of Nazareth passeth by!:||

4 But if you still this call refuse,
  And dare such wondrous love abuse,
  Soon will He sadly from you turn,
  Your bitter prayer in justice spurn:
  ||:"Too late! too late!" will be the cry,
  "Jesus of Nazareth *has passed by*.":||

139 Olivet. 6. 4.

1 My faith looks up to Thee,
    Thou Lamb of Calvary,
        Savior divine,
  Now hear me while I pray;
  Take all my guilt away;
    O let me from this day
        Be wholly thine.

2 May thy rich grace impart
    Strength to my fainting heart,
        My zeal inspire;
  As thou hast died for me,
  Oh may my love to thee
    Pure, warm and changeless be,
        A living fire.

3 While life's dark maze I tread,
    And griefs around me spread,
        Be thou my guide;
  Bid darkness turn to day,
  Wipe sorrow's tears away
    Nor let me ever stray
        From thee aside.

4 When ends life's transient dream,
    When death's cold, sullen stream
        Shall o'er me roll;
  Blest Savior, then, in love,
  Fear and distrust remove;
    Oh bear me safe above—
        A ransomed soul.

140 Go and tell Jesus.

1 Go and tell Jesus, weary, sin-sick soul,
  He'll ease thee of thy burden, make thee whole,
  Look up to him, he only can forgive,
  Believe on him and thou shalt surely live.

CHORUS:

Go and tell Jesus, he only can forgive,
Go and tell Jesus, oh turn to him and live;
Go and tell Jesus, go and tell Jesus,
Go and tell Jesus, he only can forgive.

2 Go and tell Jesus, when your sins arise
  Like mountains of deep guilt before your eyes;
  His blood was spilt, his precious life he gave,
  That mercy, peace, and pardon you might have.

3 Go and tell Jesus, he'll dispel thy fears,
  Will calm thy doubts, and wipe away thy tears;
  He'll take thee in his arms, and on his breast
  Thou may'st be happy, and forever rest.

141 Dennis. S. M.

1 Oh cease, my wandering soul,
    On restless wing to roam,
  All this wide world, to either pole
    Hath not for thee a home.

2 Behold the ark of God,
    Behold the open door,
  Oh haste to gain that dear abode,
    And rove, my soul, no more.

3 There safe thou shalt abide,
    There sweet shall be thy rest,
  And every longing satisfied,
    With full salvation blest.

142 Boylston. S. M.

1 A charge to keep I have,
    A God to glorify,
  A never-dying soul to save,
    And fit it for the sky.

2 To serve the present age,
    My calling to fulfill.
  Oh, may it all my powers engage
    To do my Master's will.

3 Arm me with jealous care,
    As in thy sight to live,
  And oh, thy servant, Lord, prepare
    A strict account to give.

4 Help me to watch and pray,
    And on thyself rely,
  Assured, if I my trust betray,
    I shall forever die.

143 Webb. 7. 6.

1 The morning light is breaking,
    The darkness disappears;
  The sons of earth are waking
    To penitential tears.
  Each breeze that sweeps the ocean
    Brings tidings from afar,
  Of nations in commotion,
    Prepared for Zion's war.

2 Rich dews of grace come o'er us,
    In many a gentle shower,
  And brighter scenes before us
    Are opening every hour.
  Each cry, to heaven going,
    Abundant answer brings,
  And heavenly gales are blowing,
    With peace upon their wings.

144   Loving Kindness.   L. M.

1 Awake, my soul, in joyful lays,
   And sing thy great Redeemer's praise;
   He justly claims a song from me;
   His loving kindness, oh, how free!

2 He saw me ruined in the fall,
   Yet loved me notwithstanding all;
   He saved me from my lost estate;
   His loving kindness, oh, how great!

3 Often I feel my sinful heart
   Prone from my Jesus to depart;
   But though I have him oft forgot,
   His loving kindness changes not.

145   Portuguese Hymn.   11.

1 How firm a foundation, ye saints of
    the Lord,
  Is laid for your faith in his excellent
    word;
  What more can he say than to you he
    hath said—
  To you who for refuge to Jesus have
    fled!

2 The soul that on Jesus hath leaned for
    repose,
  I will not—I will not desert to his foes;
  That soul—though all hell should en-
    deavor to shake,
  Jehovah will never, no, never forsake!

146   Watcher.   7. 6.

1 I want to be like Jesus,
   All gentle, pure, and mild;
  His seal upon my forehead,
   And owned as his dear child.
  My heart, so weak and sinful,
   All changed by grace divine,
  And all my life to serve him,
   And ever call him mine.

2 I want to do like Jesus,
   To mark each passing day,
  With deeds of love and mercy,
   Or cheer some lonely way;
  Speak gentle words of counsel,
   Avoid each secret sin,
  And to my precious Savior,
   The lost ones seek to win.

3 I want to live like Jesus,
   Whose words with love were fraught;
  I want to find his favor—
   By him be truly taught.
  Oh, then, I'm sure that ever
   His hand will guide me on,
  Until the heavenly portals
   And glory shall be won.

147   I Love to Tell the Story.

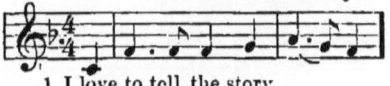

1 I love to tell the story,
   Of unseen things above,
  Of Jesus and his glory,
   Of Jesus and his love;
  I love to tell the story,
   Because I know 'tis true;
  It satisfies my longings,
   As nothing else can do.
Cho.—I love, I love to tell the story,
   'Twill be my happy theme in glory
  To tell the old, old story,
   Of Jesus and his love.

2 I love to tell the story—
   More wonderful it seems
  Than all the golden fancies
   Of all our golden dreams;
  I love to tell the story—
   It did so much for me!
  And that is just the reason
   I tell it now to thee.

3 I love to tell the story,
   "Tis pleasant to repeat
  What seems, each time I tell it,
   More wonderfully sweet;
  I love to tell the story,
   For some have never heard
  The message of salvation
   From God's own holy word.

4 I love to tell the story,
   For those who know it best
  Seem hungering and thirsting
   To hear it like the rest.
  And when, in scenes of glory,
   I sing the New, New Song,
  'Twill be the Old, Old Story,
   That I have loved so long.

148   Beautiful River.

1 Shall we gather at the river,
   Where bright angel feet have trod;
  With its crystal tide forever
   Flowing by the throne of God?
Cho.—Yes, we'll gather at the river,
   The beautiful, the beautiful river,
  Gather with the saints at the river
   That flows by the throne of God.

2 On the margin of the river,
   Washing up its silver spray,
  We will walk and worship ever,
   All the happy, golden day.

3 Ere we reach the shining river,
   Lay we every burden down;
  Grace our spirits will deliver,
   And provide a robe and crown.

4 Soon we'll reach the shining river,
   Soon our pilgrimage will cease;
  Soon our happy hearts will quiver
   With the melody of peace.

149   No sorrow there.   S. M.

1 Come, we that love the Lord,
   And let our joys be known;
Join in a song with sweet accord,
   And thus surround the throne.

2 The hill of Zion yields
   A thousand sacred sweets,
Before we reach the heavenly fields,
   Or walk the golden streets.

3 Then let our songs abound,
   And every tear be dry;
We're march'g thro' Immanuel's ground
   To fairer worlds on high.

150   Happy day.

1 Oh happy day that fixed my choice
   On thee, my Savior and my God!
Well may this glowing heart rejoice,
   And tell its raptures all abroad.

2 Oh happy bond that seals my vows
   To him that merits all my love;
Let cheerful anthems fill his house,
   While to that sacred shrine I move.

3 'Tis done, the great transaction's done;
   I am my Lord's and he is mine;
He drew me, and I follow'd on,
   Charmed to confess the voice divine.

151   Missionary Hymn.   7,6.

1 From Greenland's icy mountains,
   From India's coral strand,
Where Afric's sunny fountains
   Roll down their golden sand,
From many an ancient river,
   From many a palmy plain
They call us to deliver
   Their land from error's chain.

2 Shall we, whose souls are lighted
   With wisdom from on high,
Shall we to men benighted
   The lamp of life deny?
Salvation! oh, salvation!
   The joyful sound proclaim,
Till earth's remotest nation
   Has learned Messiah's name.

3 Waft, waft, ye winds, his story,
   And you, ye waters, roll,
Till, like a sea of glory,
   It spreads from pole to pole;
Till o'er our ransomed nature
   The Lamb, for sinners slain,
Redeemer, King, Creator,
   In bliss returns to reign.

152   Olmutz.   S. M.

1 I love thy kingdom, Lord,
   The house of thine abode,
The church our blest Redeemer saved
   With his own precious blood.

2 I love thy church, O God,
   Her walls before thee stand,
Dear as the apple of thine eye,
   And graven on thy hand.

3 For her my tears shall fall,
   For her my prayers ascend—
To her my cares and toils be given,
   Till toils and cares shall end.

4 Beyond my highest joy
   I prize her heavenly ways,
Her sweet communion, solemn vows,
   Her hymns of love and praise.

153   I will Sing for Jesus.

1 I will sing for Jesus,
   With his blood he bought me;
And all along my pilgrim way,
   His loving hand has brought me.

2 Can there overtake me
   Any dark disaster,
While I sing for Jesus,
   My blessed, blessed Master?

3 I will sing for Jesus,
   His name alone prevailing,
Shall be my sweetest music
   When heart and flesh are failing.

4 Still I'll sing for Jesus,
   Oh, how will I adore him!
Among the cloud of witnesses
   Who cast their crowns before him.

154   Depths of Mercy.   7.

1 Depth of mercy, can there be
Mercy still reserved for me?
Can my God his wrath forbear?
Me, the chief of sinners, spare?

Cho.—God is love! I know, I feel
   Jesus lives and love's me still—
   Jesus lives, he lives and loves me still.

2 I have long withstood his grace,
Long provoked him to his face,
Would not hearken to his calls,
Grieved him by a thousand falls.

3 Now incline me to repent,
Let me now my sins lament;
Now my foul revolt deplore,
Weep, believe and sin no more.

155 Christmas. C. M.

1 Awake, my soul, stretch every nerve,
   And press with vigor on;
A heavenly race demands thy zeal,
   And an immortal crown.

2 A cloud of witnesses around
   Hold thee in full survey;
Forget the steps already trod,
   And onward urge thy way.

3 'Tis God's all-animating voice
   That calls thee from on high—
'Tis his own hand presents the prize
   To thine aspiring eye.

156 Never be afraid.

1 Never be afraid to speak for Jesus,
   Think how much a word can do;
Never be afraid to own your Savior,
   He who loves and cares for you.

Cho.—Never be afraid,
   Never be afraid,
   Never, never, never;
Jesus is your loving Savior,
   Therefore never be afraid.

2 Never be afraid to work for Jesus,
   In his vineyard day by day,
Labor with a kind and willing spirit,
   He will all your toil repay.
   Never be afraid, etc.

3 Never be afraid to die for Jesus,
   He the life, the truth, the way,
Gently in his arms of love will bear you
   To the realms of endless day.
   Never be afraid, etc.

157 Work for the night.

1 Work, for the night is coming,
   Work thro' the morning hours;
Work while the dew is sparkling,
   Work 'mid springing flowers;
Work when the day grows brighter,
   Work in the glowing sun,
Work for the night is coming,
   When man's work is done.

2 Work, for the night is coming,
   Work thro' the sunny noon,
Fill brightest hours with labor,
   Rest comes sure and soon.
Give every flying minute
   Something to keep in store:
Work, for the night is coming,
   When man works no more.

158 The Lord will provide.

1 In some way or other
   The Lord will provide;
It may not be *my* way,
It may not be *thy* way,
And yet, in his *own* way,
   The Lord will provide.

Cho.—It may not be *my* way,
   It may not be *thy* way,
   And yet, in his *own* way
   The Lord will provide.

2 At some time or other
   The Lord will provide;
It may not be *my* time,
It may not be *thy* time,
And yet, in his *own* time,
   The Lord will provide.

3 Despond, then, no longer,
   The Lord will provide;
And this be the token—
No word he hath spoken
Was ever yet broken—
   The Lord will provide.

159 The Heavenly land.

1 I love to think of the heavenly land,
   Where white-robed angels are;
Where many a friend is gathered safe
   From fear, and toil, and care.

Ref.—There'll be no parting,
   There'll be no parting,
   There'll be no parting,
   There'll be no parting there.

2 I love to think of the heavenly land,
   Where my Redeemer reigns.
Where rapturous songs of triumph rise
   In endless, joyous strains.

3 I love to think of the heavenly land,
   The saints' eternal home,
Where palms, and robes, and crowns ne'er fade,
   And all our joys are one.

160 Ortonville. C. M.

1 Come, humble sinner, in whose breast
   A thousand thoughts revolve,
Come, with your guilt and fear oppres'd,
   And make this last resolve:

2 I'll go to Jesus, though my sin
   Like mountains round me close;
I know his courts, I'll enter in,
   Whatever may oppose.

161 Your Mission.

1 Hark! the voice of Jesus, crying,
  Who will go and work to-day?
  Fields are white and harvests waiting,
  Who will bear the sheaves away?
  Loud and long the Master calleth,
  Rich reward he offers free;
  Who will answer, gladly saying,
  "Here am I, send me, send me?"

2 If you can not cross the ocean,
  And the heathen lands explore,
  You can find the heathen nearer,
  You can help them at your door.
  If you can not give your thousands,
  You can give the widow's mite;
  And the least you give for Jesus,
  Will be precious in his sight.

3 While the souls of men are dying,
  And the Master calls for you,
  Let none hear you idly saying,
  "There is nothing I can do!"
  Take the task he gives you gladly,
  Let his work your pleasure be;
  Answer quickly when he calleth,
  "Here am I, send me, send me!"

162 Am I a Soldier? C. M.

1 Am I a soldier of the cross,
  A follower of the Lamb;
  And shall I fear to own his cause,
  Or blush to speak his name?

  CHORUS.
  Let us never mind the scoffs nor the frowns of the world,
  For we all have the cross to bear;
  It will only make the crown the brighter to shine,
  When we have the crown to wear.

2 Must I be carried to the skies
  On flowery beds of ease,
  While others fought to win the prize,
  And sailed through bloody seas?

3 Are there no foes for me to face,
  Must I not stem the flood?
  Is this vile world a friend to grace,
  To help me on to God?

163 I do Believe. C. M.

1 How sweet the name of Jesus sounds
  In a believer's ear!
  It soothes his sorrows, heals his wounds,
  And drives away his fear.

  CHO.—I do believe, I now believe,
  That Jesus died for me;
  And thro' his blood, his precious blood,
  I shall from sin be free.

164 Federal Street. L. M.

1 Jesus, and shall it ever be,
  A mortal man ashamed of thee!
  Ashamed of thee whom angels praise,
  Whose glories shine thro' endless days.

2 Ashamed of Jesus! that dear Friend
  On whom my hopes of heaven depend!
  No! when I blush be this my shame—
  That I no more revere his name.

3 Ashamed of Jesus! yes, I may,
  When I've no guilt to wash away,
  No tear to wipe, no good to crave,
  No fears to quell, no soul to save.

165 Webb. 7. 6.

1 Stand up, stand up for Jesus,
  Ye soldiers of the cross,
  Lift high his royal banner,
  It must not suffer loss;
  From vict'ry unto vict'ry,
  His army shall he lead,
  Till every foe is vanquished,
  And Christ is Lord indeed.

2 Stand up, stand up for Jesus,
  Stand in his strength alone;
  The arm of flesh will fail you,
  Ye dare not trust your own.
  Put on the gospel armor,
  And watching unto prayer,
  Where duty calls, or danger,
  Be never wanting there.

3 Stand up, stand up for Jesus,
  The strife will not be long;
  This day the noise of battle,
  The next the victor's song.
  To him that overcometh
  A crown of life shall be;
  He with the King of glory
  Shall reign eternally.

166 Autumn. 8. 7.

1 In the cross of Christ I glory,
  Towering o'er the wrecks of time;
  All the light of sacred story
  Gathers round its head sublime.
  When the woes of life o'ertake me,
  Hopes deceive and fears annoy,
  Never shall the cross forsake me;
  Lo! it glows with peace and joy.

2 When the sun of bliss is beaming
  Light and love upon my way,
  From the cross the radiance streaming
  Adds new luster to the day.
  Bane and blessing, pain and pleasure
  By the cross are sanctified;
  Peace is there that knows no measure,
  Joys that through all time abide.

INDEX.

Titles in SMALL CAPS, First lines in Roman.

	No.
A CHARGE to keep I have	142
A few more prayers	63
A few more sweet communings	93
ALAS! AND DID MY SAVIOR BLEED	83
ALL HAIL THE POWER	103
AMAZING GRACE	78
Am I a soldier of the cross	162
ANYWHERE WITH THEE	20
Awake, my soul, in joyful lays	144
Awake, my soul, stretch every	155
BEAR THE CROSS FOR JESUS	33
BEHOLD A STRANGER AT THE	107
Blessed Jesus, blessed Jesus	2
BLEST BE THE TIE	112
Brighter and brighter the way	64
Brightly beams our Father's mercy	56
Bright till our Lord's returning	17
BRING THY ALL TO JESUS	35
BROAD IS THE ROAD	106
CAST YOUR CARE ON JESUS	38
Cast your care on Jesus	77
Close the heart to all but Jesus	35
Come away, O ye thirsty	46
Come, come to Jesus	59
Come Holy Spirit, heavenly Dove	132
Come home, come home	69
Come, humble sinner, in whose	160
COME IN OUR MIDST	48
COME! SAID JESUS	113
Come, talk to me of Jesus	89
COME, THOU FOUNT	102
COME TO JESUS	99
Come, we that love the Lord	149
Come, ye sinners, poor and needy	119
CONSECRATE ME, LORD	94
CROWN OF LIFE	41

	No.
DEPTH of mercy, can there be	154
Did Christ o'er sinners weep	122
DRAW ME NEARER	30
Draw nearer, my Savior	60
EVERY DAY AND HOUR	90
FATHER, I stretch my hands	127
Father, whate'er of earthly	125
FROM EVERY STORMY WIND	108
From Greenland's icy mountains	151
From the hundred sheep	68
GLAD TIDINGS	24
Gracious Spirit, love divine	86
GIVE THY HEART to ME	71
Go and tell Jesus	140
God's tender mercy far exceeds	11
HAD earth no thorns among	92
HALLELUJAH! WHO SHALL	85
Hark! there comes a whisper	71
Hark! the voice of Jesus, crying	161
Haste, O sinner, now be wise	118
Hast Thou, my Master, aught	52
HE IS COMING OUT TO MEET US	36
He leadeth me	130
Helpless I come to Jesus' blood	55
Here from the world we turn	1
HOLD IT UP TO THE WORLD	57
How firm a foundation	145
How sweet the name of Jesus	163
I AM coming to the cross	115
I AM SAVED	42
I am thine, O Lord	30
I AM TRUSTING, LORD, IN THEE	115
I COME TO THEE	5

INDEX.

	No.		No.
I gave my life for thee	51	My faith looks up to Thee	139
I LOVE THEE	82	MY FAITH STILL CLINGS	39
I love thy kingdom, Lord	152	My hope is built on nothing less	126
I LOVE TO HEAR OF JESUS	88	My Jesus, I love Thee	129
I love to tell the story	147	My sin is great, my strength is weak	39
I love to think of the heavenly	159	MY SOUL WILL OVERCOME	55
I NEED THEE EVERY HOUR	58		
In some way or other	158	NEARER, my God, to Thee	124
IN THAT HAPPY LAND	98	NEAR THE CROSS	74
In the cross of Christ I glory	166	Never be afraid to speak for Jesus	156
IN THE VALLEY	63	NO ONE KNOWS BUT JESUS	13
IN TIME OF NEED	25	NOTHING BUT THE BLOOD OF JESUS	7
Is there trouble in your life	38	Now just a word for Jesus	19
I want to be like Jesus	146	NOW THE SAVIOR INVITES	43
I want to live for Jesus	66		
I WILL GO AND TELL MY SAVIOR	27	OH, cease, my wandering soul	141
I will sing for Jesus	153	OH, COME AND WORK FOR	40
		OH, COME TO CHRIST	28
JESUS, and shall it ever be	164	Oh, could I find, from day to day	136
JESUS CALLS THEE	29	OH, FOR A CLOSER WALK	109
Jesus, gracious One	29	Oh, for a faith that will not shrink	123
JESUS, I TURN TO THEE	45	Oh, happy day that fixed my	150
Jesus, keep me near the cross	74	OH, TO BE NOTHING	73
JESUS, LOVER OF MY SOUL	110	OH, TURN YE, OH, TURN YE	114
JESUS ONLY	18	OH, LAMB OF GOD, STILL KEEP ME	97
Jesus the water of life will give	137	O Lord! awakened by thy word	5
JESUS WAITS FOR THEE	59	Oh, meek and gentle Savior	8
JUST AS I AM	105	ONE MORE DAY'S WORK FOR JESUS	31
JUST A WORD FOR JESUS	19	ONLY A STEP TO JESUS	22
		ONLY JESUS	4
KEEP ME, LORD, FOREVER	86	Only Thee, my soul's Redeemer	88
		OUR BETTER HOME BEYOND	92
LEAD ME TO JESUS	80	OVERFLOWING EVER	14
LET THE LOWER LIGHTS BE	56	OVER THE OCEAN WAVE	62
Lift up thine eyes, weary pris'ner	6		
LINGER NO LONGER	21	PASS ME NOT	79
LIVING FOR JESUS	66	Press on, pilgrim, young tho'	41
Lo! a fountain, full and free	14		
Lo! an ever-flowing fountain	3	REACH ME THY HAND	96
LORD, AT THY MERCY SEAT	61	RESCUE THE PERISHING	84
Lord, I hear of showers of blessings	133	REST IN THEE	2
LOVING SAVIOR, ONLY THEE	88	ROCK OF AGES	111
MASTER, in the vineyard of thy	20	SAFE IN THE ARMS OF JESUS	54
MORE FAITHFUL TO THEE	60	SAVE, OR I PERISH	10
MORE LIKE JESUS	67	Savior, like a shepherd lead us	131
MORE LOVE TO THEE, O CHRIST	76	Savior, more than life to me	90
Must Jesus bear the cross alone	117	SAVIOR, WE WAIT FOR THEE	81

INDEX.

	No.
Shall we gather at the river	148
Show pity, Lord, O Lord forgive	135
Simply trusting all the way	15
SO NEAR TO THE KINGDOM	53
SPEAK FOR JESUS	12
Stand up, stand up for Jesus	165
Sweet hour of prayer	128
SWEET MOMENTS OF PRAYER	1
TAKE my life and let it be	94
Take the cross, take the cross	57
Take the name of Jesus with you	37
TAKE THE WINGS OF THE MORNING	16
TELL IT WITH JOY	65
TELL ME THE OLD, OLD STORY	95
THE HALF CAN NEVER BE TOLD	11
THE HEM OF HIS GARMENT	49
THE LIVING FOUNTAIN	3
THE LOST SHEEP	68
THE MISTAKES OF MY LIFE	50
The morning light is breaking	143
THE PENITENT'S PRAYER	8
THE PRECIOUS NAME	37
THE PRODIGAL CHILD	69
THERE ARE ANGELS HOV'RING	72
THERE IS A FOUNTAIN	100
THERE IS A NAME I LOVE	104
There is no name so sweet on earth	134
THERE IS NONE LIKE JESUS	77
THERE'LL BE JOY BY AND BY	47
THERE'S A GENTLE VOICE	9
THERE'S A SONG IN HEAVEN FOR	34
The Spirit in our hearts	121

	No.
THE VOICE OF MERCY	6
Tho' the mist hangs o'er the river	120
Tho' the night be dark and dreary	47
THO' YOUR SINS BE AS SCARLET	44
TILL THE SAVIOR COMES	17
TO-DAY THE SAVIOR CALLS	70
TRUSTING JESUS	15
WAITING AND WATCHING FOR	87
Weak and weary, poor and	49
We are traveling home	98
WEARY ONE, WAND'RING ONE	75
WEEPING WILL NOT SAVE ME	91
WE'LL MEET AGAIN	93
WE PRAISE THEE, O GOD	101
Were it not for Thee, my Savior	25
WE WILL JOURNEY ON	64
What a friend we have in Jesus	116
What can wash away my stain	7
WHAT HAST THOU DONE FOR ME	51
What means this eager, anxious	138
What tho' clouds are hov'ring o'er	18
When Jesus comes to reward	32
When my final farewell	87
When we turn to God and leave	36
WHERE SHALL I WORK TO-DAY	54
WHO'LL BE THE NEXT	23
WHOSOEVER WILL	46
WHY WEEPEST THOU	26
WILL JESUS FIND US WATCHING	32
Work, for the night is coming	157
Wrecked on the billow	10

www.ingramcontent.com/pod-product-compliance
Lightning Source LLC
Chambersburg PA
CBHW020142170426
43199CB00010B/843